For Jocelyn and London,
the past and the future

PRAISE FOR *HOW TO GET SH*T DONE*

"Erin Falconer is a renowned name in the field of lifestyle and self-improvement."

—*Business Wire*

"The timing for this book could not be more perfect. Not only is it empowering and inspirational for women, it also helps you realign the definition of personal productivity with what real success looks like in three simple steps. Highly recommended."

—Alexia Brue, cofounder and CEO of *Well+Good*

"If you're looking to be more productive this year, Erin Falconer might be able to show you the way."

—*Bustle*

"If you swear every year will be the year you finally finish your endless to-do lists and become a productivity machine, this book is for you."

—Today.com

"As someone who is constantly trying to be as productive as possible, *How to Get Sh*t Done* is a game changer. Employing simple tactics that focus on the root of who you are (as an individual and as a woman) and where you want to go, this book informs not on how to get more done, but on how to do less and achieve more."

—Jaclyn Johnson, founder and CEO of *Create & Cultivate*

✓ HOW
✓ TO GET
✓ SH*T
✓ DONE

**WHY WOMEN NEED TO STOP DOING EVERYTHING
SO THEY CAN ACHIEVE ANYTHING**

Erin Falconer

G

GALLERY BOOKS

New York   London   Toronto   Sydney   New Delhi

G

Gallery Books
An Imprint of Simon & Schuster, Inc.
1230 Avenue of the Americas
New York, NY 10020

First Gallery Books trade paperback edition January 2019

GALLERY BOOKS and colophon are registered trademarks of Simon & Schuster, Inc.

Certain names and identifying characteristics have been changed.

For information about special discounts for bulk purchases, please contact Simon & Schuster Special Sales at 1-866-506-1949 or business@simonandschuster.com.

The Simon & Schuster Speakers Bureau can bring authors to your live event. For more information or to book an event, contact the Simon & Schuster Speakers Bureau at 1-866-248-3049 or visit our website at www.simonspeakers.com.

Interior design by Davina Mock-Maniscalco

Manufactured in the United States of America

10   9   8   7   6   5

The Library of Congress has cataloged the hardcover edition as follows:

Names: Falconer, Erin, author.
Title: How to get sh*t done : why women need to stop doing everything so they can achieve anything / by Erin Falconer.
Other titles: How to get shit done
Description: New York, NY : North Star Way, [2018]
Identifiers: LCCN 2017036021 (print) | LCCN 2017045585 (ebook) | ISBN 9781501165795 (ebook) | ISBN 9781501165788 (hardcover)
Subjects: LCSH: Self-realization in women. | Time management. | Work. | Success.
Classification: LCC HQ1206 (ebook) | LCC HQ1206 .F173 2018 (print) | DDC 158.1082—dc23
LC record available at https://lccn.loc.gov/2017036021

ISBN 978-1-5011-6578-8
ISBN 978-1-5011-6580-1 (pbk)
ISBN 978-1-5011-6579-5 (ebook)

Contents

✓ HOW
✓ TO GET
✓ SH*T
✓ DONE

Who Am I?

From the age of five until I graduated grade twelve, I went to the best private girls' school in Winnipeg, Manitoba: Balmoral Hall. In grade nine, the best private boys' school decided to let girls in. So I lost a third of my classmates, because naturally, the boys' school was considered better. *Wamp-wamp.*

I was elected head girl. I was captain of the debate team. I graduated valedictorian. I went to the Oxford University summer program on a full scholarship. I played the sax.

The spring of my senior year I started doing stand-up comedy.

Shock was only outweighed by outrage, then, when I was *wait-listed*(!) at Harvard—*should I have gone to that stupid bloody boys' school?!*

And so I decided to do McGill—Canada's Harvard—a favor and show up there instead. Shock was only outweighed by outrage once again, when McGill let me know it didn't give a shit that I was there—a fact that was duly reflected in my B– first-year grades.

Undeterred, I doubled down on my studies. Learned how to smoke Gauloises cigarettes. Dated an Asian, an Israeli, and an Arab (there's a joke in there somewhere). You could say I got cosmopolitan—*fast*. For the first time, I fell in love with a city and with poutine, and graduated with honors. I slayed my LSATs and was on the fast track to law school when I stopped and said to myself, *Why make things easy?*

So I moved to Toronto to become a writer.

With the firm knowledge that their daughter would lose sleep for a week if she scored less than 90 percent on anything including an eye exam, my parents were cautiously supportive, taking comfort in the fact that this act of joie de vivre would be a creative, fulfilling experiment that would, most definitely, end a year later with my acceptance into Osgoode Hall Law School.

Five years later, I sat across from my parents in a Toronto café—Eggspectation—bleary-eyed from another long, fun night of bartending. They'd flown in for a polite, Canadian-style intervention. I recall my dad, a worried look on his face, saying, "You've given this enough time here."

"I agree!" I said, with all the confidence in the world. A relieved, I-knew-she'd-start-thinking-rationally-again smile graced both my parents' faces. "That's why I've decided that, if I really want to give this dream a chance, I need to move to Los Angeles," I announced proudly.

And coffee was spat across the table.

Three days after 9/11, I flew back to Winnipeg, jumped in my parents' old Camry, and drove across the border straight down to L.A.

I had no money—C$700, to be exact. I had no papers. And no clue.

The next ten years were a total roller coaster. I worked a string of odd jobs. I finally got my working visa because my education gave me special status (thank God for Canada's Harvard!), and my parents mentioned my law career with less and less frequency. Things were looking good. I wrote five scripts, made two festival-nominated short films, rollerbladed on the boardwalk, lived in Venice Beach, fell madly in love, and became an honorary Angeleno. Everything was perfect. Until it wasn't.

About five years in, I suffered a major personal tragedy (that is a book unto itself). A year later, in 2008, the economy crashed. My partner and I lost everything.

We broke up.

I didn't have a car.

My house was being foreclosed upon.

My visa was up.

I was destroyed.

The words of my father screamed over and over in my head: *"You've given this enough time. YOU'VE GIVEN THIS ENOUGH TIME!"* I had completely messed up. If there was some path I was supposed to be on, I hadn't gotten the memo. Or maybe I'd got it and ignored it. My whole life I had followed that little voice in my head telling me to go for it. As I looked at my "ninety days to vacate" letter from the bank, it seemed that voice had failed me.

I had wanted to show the world the person I knew was inside me, that ambitious chick who takes on the world. Instead, I was incapable of doing a single damn thing right. Even worse, I could barely find, much less pick up the pieces of, myself. I just didn't know who I was anymore, but I sure wasn't that confidence-of-ten-men girl I used to be.

So I gave up, put my tail between my legs, and planned my humiliating retreat to my parents' house in Canada, complete with YOU TOLD ME SO tattooed on my forehead. I had to accept that I obviously wasn't destined to conquer L.A. I could barely pay my rent, much less make it as a writer. Sobbing, I started to pack up my life, readying for the move.

And in that lowest moment, my life started to take a turn.

Here's what I know to be true: *If you want to make God laugh, tell Him your plans.*

I had put in one last hail-Mary application for a copywriting job I'd seen on Craigslist—and I got it. It was a steady writing gig at a small, self-development start-up that paid $15 an hour. At first, this seemed like an incredible blow to my ego. It was not exactly the type of writing job I had envisioned for myself when I'd made the move to L.A. *That* writing job had involved George Clooney handing me my Oscar and his number. It wasn't awesome, it wasn't epic, but these were dire straits and I needed to buy some time.

I threw everything I had into that job, and it turned out I was pretty good at it. Actually, I ended up being amazing at it. I did good work, I made connections, and I learned about the internet. I took over a small blog called *Pick the Brain*, and as it began to really grow, I did, too. Within two years, *PTB* was one of the most successful self-development sites on the web and I was the editor in chief and co-owner. Eventually, I realized that I *was* living the dream: I was paying the rent with my words! What I hadn't expected was how much I ended up learning from the hundreds of self-development writers I was editing and managing. I couldn't have known when I started that we'd end up helping other people to not make the shitty decisions I'd made. It felt really, really, really good to help other people find their way.

As the years passed, another transformation began. I started remembering that confidence-of-ten-men girl I used to be before life kicked me in the face. I was spending a huge chunk of my workday reading self-improvement content by people who were much smarter than me, and hell, it was working. *Pick the Brain* literally helped me pick up the pieces of my life and get back into the mind-set that I needed to shake off the sad-sack, always-apologizing, always-afraid girl I'd become in my early twenties. It taught me how to get shit done and to not give a damn if I didn't prioritize the things everyone else wanted me to.

Two years later, I raised close to a million dollars with my partner, Geri Hirsch, to launch our own lifestyle start-up, the first in-video shopping site on the web, called LEAFtv. I had more than three hundred writers from around the world writing for *Pick the Brain*. *Forbes* magazine ranked the blog as one of "The Top 100 Most Influential Sites for Women, 2013."

Two years later still, LEAF was bought by publicly traded Demand Media. Geri and I were "acquired" for two years as part of the deal.

I was killing it.

Or was I . . . ?

———

So about two years ago, I was juggling two successful companies in a business that never sleeps, when a fancy New York literary agent hit me up inquiring as to whether I had any interest in writing a book.

Did I want to write a book?!

UMMMM. HELLO, GOD, IT'S ME, MARGARET!

This was only the whole, entire reason I'd moved to Los Angeles in the first place.

But how could I possibly get this done? What was the cruelest of ironies? They wanted me to write a book on productivity! I found myself in a real predicament.

I'd have to find the time.

We signed the paperwork, and thirteen years after moving to L.A., I was officially a repped writer. *I couldn't believe it.*

Seven long months dragged on. I hadn't written a word. Not. A. Word.

To my surprise, the enthusiasm from New York hadn't dwindled— if anything, it intensified. They wouldn't let me off the hook. I began to beat myself up. How could I let this opportunity slip away? How could I not get this done? *Me?!*

One month later and I was just about to throw in the towel. I had a phone meeting scheduled with my agent to go over my latest lame musings for the book on productivity that I couldn't start. *Ironic much?* What I really planned to tell her was that now just wasn't the right time. I'd have to give up.

And I would have, if I hadn't read one email shortly before my call.

Every month, being alumni of the best girls' school in Winnipeg means I get a newsletter with the subject line *Calling All Crestlines*, which, loosely translated, means, "Write us and let us know of what successes you've had in life." I had been receiving these monthly emails for the past three or four years. And every month I would open them and look at all the achievements of past students:

> "Mary Joe Clairmont, née Smith, '96, has just welcomed her first child, Max"; "Barbara Goldberg, née Rosen, '99, was accepted into the Masters of Engineering Program at Dalhousie"; "Ginnie Rotthousen, née Flugelsteen, '57, has successfully house-trained her new Golden Retriever."*

---

* These are not actual Crestlines, but you get the point.

And every month for three or four years, I would say to myself, *I can't wait for the day when I'll have something to report. Maybe next month!*

Well, shortly before I was to dial-in for the call with my agent, the monthly *Calling All Crestlines* newsletter popped up on my screen, and, like clockwork, I scrolled through the tributes and began to say, *I can't wait for the day when I'll have something to report*—when I stopped myself short.

"Are you kidding me?" I said out loud.

You wish you had something to report?

How about something like, oh, I don't know:

You have one of the most respected self-improvement blogs on the planet, you sold your start-up after only two years in business to a publicly traded company (which is now trading as the Leaf Group on the Dow), you made a *Forbes* top 100 list, you have been named one of the top digital influencers in Los Angeles, you now have four hundred people writing for you, you've been invited to give two TEDx talks, you have over ONE MILLION people following you on social networks . . .

And as I was listing all this stuff—*and should have felt great!*—I instead started to realize how tired I was, how relatively unhappy I was. I hadn't been giving myself credit for everything (*or anything*) that I'd accomplished. And maybe I wasn't really valuing the things I'd managed to do. There was clearly no retrospection—it was always just on to the next, on to the next! In other words, I was as productive as hell, but not on my own terms.

And that's when it hit me.

I was going to start over. *Again.* I was going to figure out what mattered to me, how to get things done while being authentic to my values and goals as a person and as a woman. I knew it might take a while, but I also knew I was onto something. And because I'm nothing if not ambitious, I had a feeling I could come up with a path to productivity that other women could use, too.

I called up my agent, new excitement in my voice.

Yes, I would write this book!

And yes, it would be on productivity!

Calling All Crestlines: Erin Falconer, née Falconer, '92, will write a book redefining feminine productivity in the twenty-first century.

Read all about it.

If you can find the time . . .

PART ONE

Being

The Power of POP

CHAPTER ONE

Defining POP (Personality, Opportunity, Productivity)

F reud once asked, "What do women want?"

Good. Fucking. Question.

What interests me most about this is that men seem to pose this question with great frequency, and yet it barely crosses the mind of most women. Or when it does, it comes laden with guilt—*I can't waste my time thinking about this when I could be, should be, getting more done!* Women are, in the classic sense of the word, the very definition of productive. I can't think of a species (other than the leaf-cutter ant) that has gotten more stuff done—let's start with the creation and the survival of the entire human race, for example—and yet, somehow, *somehow*, up until very recently, women have been viewed, most jarringly from our own lens, as *less-than*. We have a constant need to prove our worth, when our worth should be obvious to anyone or anything living within a hundred-mile radius of planet earth.

We're getting a lot done, right? More and more, every day, with every new app, and every new convenience. Except these modern conveniences (which particularly benefit women—I'll talk about this later) should probably be used to free up time, so you can, you know, have a life. But instead, women being women, how are they being used? Oh, we're saving time, all right. Saving time to get more stuff done.

Studies show that on average, women spend one to three hours more each day working than men, when you take into account unpaid work at home. That's right: you're putting in a full day at your paid job (although you're only paid 80 cents on the dollar compared to your male colleague) and then you head home to clock a few more hours looking after kids, getting dinner ready, and doing laundry. And doesn't it feel like the more we're getting done, the more unhappy, manic, and stressed we are? Sure, there's the initial high you get from making it through your daily to-do list. But it's like a drug—that high is fleeting, and we're left at the end of the day exhausted, with aching backs from all that leaning in.

It's preposterous.

So why is this happening? How is it that we're busier than ever, yet feeling like we're not getting anywhere? Here's what I think: many of us don't know what makes us happy. Or that we deserve a happiness that's worth investigating. Moreover, we're not taking the time to analyze what course of action is the right one to bring out the best version of ourselves. Sure, we might have ideas about what we like, what gives us pleasure ("Friday nights with pizza, wine, and my girls" or "Watching my kids explore the world"), but we haven't spent time zeroing in on what it would take for us to be truly happy and satisfied, what gives us energy vs. takes, and how those findings should dictate our future behavior. Without this sense of fulfillment—and real, intentional purpose—true "productivity" will be always out of reach.

I mean, I get it. In life, we're judged according to what we've done. And women are consistently assessed more harshly. A New York University study showed that women have to do much more than men to be perceived as equally productive in the workplace. So we keep chugging along. "Me? I'm *great*. I got so much done today!" We want to have spotless homes, healthy-yet-gourmet meals, executive-track promotions, well-behaved children, a robust spiritual life, spotless community service, hot sex, and, on top of all that, some time to relax. But herein lies the conundrum. If we continue to pursue productivity for productivity's sake, women will continue to position ourselves diametrically opposed to satisfaction.

You may feel like the most productive person alive, but without a purpose, *you're just busy.*

THE BACKSTORY

I think it's important to briefly explore this history and just how we got here and our relationship to productivity, success, and happiness. In a 140-character world, said history goes something like this:

Old, like really old, productivity for women meant: have a kid. If you'd done this you could die happily, I guess, at around forty-five, knowing you'd been super productive and accomplished everything anybody had ever expected of you. Done.

Except, after a time, the subconscious questions started percolating: *But if we're just fulfilling a biological imperative, where is our individual worth?* And then the questions just kept coming.

Jump-cut to today, when we have now spent many lifetimes trying to prove that we are not just the perpetuators of a biological imperative, but beings who are worth far more than even the sum of our physical strength or mental aptitude. Better. Smarter. Faster. *Because women can do it. We're not just baby-making machines.*

And then the internet came. And the other shoe dropped.

Why?

Because now the tools of power had shifted and, for the first time in history, in favor of women.

A Quick Primer on the TOP (or the Tools of Power)

The original tool of power was physical strength. Men 1, women 0. It was followed up by pursuits of the intellectual (something women were long denied participation in). Men 2, women 0. But now, the new tool of power, and the ultimate power (right after sustaining the human race, of course) is information. And man, this might just be the upset victory for the ages. Access to and the ability to share information are growing at near the speed of light. *WWW*: three letters that would not only change the world but change the game. Having information, tools to communicate, and the ability to share ideas without the traditional, hierarchical structures that previously hindered women meant entire new careers opening up. Since these careers were no longer bound to traditional roles, the playing field was leveled. And we made strides. *Major strides.* Today I am surrounded by women who are successful, productive, inspirational, and very powerful. And yet still a fog hangs above us.

WHY?

From my perspective, a lot of us are just out there frantically collecting trophies or, conversely, just trying to make it through the day. Neither is particularly fulfilling. Our world, bookshelves, and Twitter feeds are cluttered with far too much analysis on how to get more stuff done, and far too little analysis on what is necessary to feel successful and fulfilled. I don't mean that in a bullshitty, self-improvementy sort of way.

And I should know. I spend a great deal of time on my blog, lecturing people on detaching themselves from outcomes—telling them to act creatively, with integrity and with measure, to just *be* and *do*. But upon reflection, what am I recommending people do in this book? "Just go around being"? That feels a little New Agey, if I'm being frank with myself. The flip side, however, seems even less palatable: creating a rigid, endless, and impossible checklist of to-dos.

But where's the happy medium between being and doing?

If you're reading this book, I'm going to guess that you're already busy. And you certainly don't need me to tell you how to fit even more into your day. Which is great, because I'm going to do the exact opposite of that. In fact, I'm going to ask you to toss out most of your preconceived notions of busyness and success in order to help you truly get shit done.

With this book, I have, perhaps, lofty goals. A repositioning of the way we, as women, think about ourselves at work and at home. That's a big thing. It's an undoing, or a redoing, of a modern, utterly complex psychological history, wherein women have been defined by and become (a) what others think they should be or (b) a skewed version of what *we* think we should be, for far too long. We've finally come to a place where greatness is within our grasp: we've got the strength, we've got the tools—we just need to learn how to channel them in the right direction. I'm not talking about changing the rules. I'm talking about understanding them and then doing away with them entirely. I'm talking about releasing ourselves from the shackles of preconceived notions of who we are and what we should be and living in a conscious state, where only the answer to the very fundamental question below matters.

So here we go. *What do women want?*

And by women . . . I mean you.

How about we start by redefining productivity?

What I know is that the reworking of what feminine productivity should be is fundamentally necessary if a life worth living is to be achieved and sustained.

First things first: How is it possible to attain happiness, fulfillment, and a sense that we've been *truly* productive in our lives if we haven't even asked the most fundamental question of ourselves?

Who are you? What gives you energy—like, real energy? Who makes you happy? And of course, what do you really want?

These questions are daunting, not only on their surface but in their depth. They are especially difficult for women to answer, because of our long history of repression (both external and internal).

Without a thorough analysis of who we are and what we want, even with the greatest power tool at our disposal we will just burn out. And that's exactly what I am starting to see around me.

It is from this impending burnout—of which I myself was at the forefront—that I came up with the principles that could make true productivity possible. To be more precise, I came up with three tenets: **p**ersonality, **o**pportunity, **p**roductivity . . . and hence, the **POP Effect** was born.

WHAT *IS* POP?

By taking the time to analyze who we are and what really defines us—on the three abovementioned fundamental levels—we can finally begin to carve out how to be productive in life in a way that makes it all worth it. This is a system that allows for the kind of meaningful happiness and sense of satisfaction I'm talking about, by letting you really *get shit done.*

POP takes personality (**P**)—who *you* are—and combines it with where you are in life and in the world, *as a woman*, a.k.a. your opportunity (**O**), to create your very own definition of productivity (**P**). In the past, productivity gurus (usually men) have failed to take the first **P** or the **O** into consideration while urging us on to do more, more, more. But by using **POP**, you're going to redefine what being productive means to *you*. Your notion of productivity may not end up looking like anyone else's. And that's the point. Rather than following conventional notions of productivity that merely cram more into your day, what we will be doing is simplifying or removing many tangible and concrete, seemingly important (but ultimately clogging) things from your life in order to make room for the far more important, in-tangible, esoteric, and most powerful things to come in—adding a feeling of clarity and levity and a true sense of accomplishment and purpose to your world.

Here are just a few of the items we'll be shrugging off (and man, is it going to feel good):

+ Traditional definitions of productivity. It's a rigged system that was never going to work for you.

+ Your current beliefs regarding what a productive day looks like. That packed Google calendar is not your friend.

+ Impressing others in order to feel worthwhile. See "rigged system" above.

+ Doing what other people expect of you. You know what they say about putting your own oxygen mask on first? That.

Each step of the POP System, and the philosophies that support it, will be examined and explained in depth throughout the book. But for now, a quick explanation of the concepts.

WHO ARE YOU?

(P for Personality)

If we're setting out to create a sense of productivity that's tailor-made for you, we'd better start by knowing who you are. More than mere navel-gazing, deep self-knowledge is essential before creating an action plan. Skipping this step, as so many of us do, can leave us with a life that's full but that doesn't feel like our own.

I'm going to give you exercises in order to bring you and your dreams and desires into sharp focus. And it's all going to be based on a practice that may be new to you: *self-reflection*. In part, this new habit that we'll be putting into effect is simple observation. But you'll soon see the ways that it may shift some of your behaviors, particularly the ones that do you no favors.

To understand how this process looks, I spoke with Dr. Anita Chakrabarti. She's a psychiatrist with an interest in self-development. She also happens to be my stepmother, someone I'm very close to and to whom I turn to for rigorous intellectual engagement. Helping people to know themselves is Anita's life work, so of course she was one of my first stops on this journey.

Anita described the backbone of the trek toward self-knowledge as anything but a straight line.

1 *We're wild.* We may spend our lives civilizing ourselves, but there's something primal at our core. "The first thing we have to do is realize we have drives and instincts. You have to kind of accept that. Or at least consider it and give it some legitimate consideration. Because if you're doing things that are unconscious, then it's hard to make decisions. And it's really hard to make good decisions."

2 *Take note.* "The next step is trying to think and reflect about what you're doing. To me, that is the most important part of this whole process," says Anita. Your job isn't to judge but to just observe your thoughts and feelings. "In dynamic practice, we call this listening

with the third ear. It's the part of your mind that is able to step back and kind of objectively and neutrally say, 'What is it that I'm doing? What am I thinking? What am I feeling?'" There may be times in your life when you do this more actively, and go see a therapist, or there may be times when it's less pressing. But it's not a onetime exercise; rather, it's something you want to practice throughout your life.

3 *Think about it.* Once you've started making observations about yourself, you'll want to do something with that information. You can look for patterns in your life and also patterns in the world, in the shape of family or cultural expectations. "You can keep layering on the levels of sophistication," says Anita. For instance, if letting anyone down gives you an uncomfortable sting of guilt, you may feel paralyzed or drawn to old habits of obligation and resentment. "But there's another process where you say, 'Yes, I've got guilt. I've actually seen that in a whole bunch of places. Wow, that's really interesting. I'm going to keep an eye out for it because I might see it somewhere else.'" If you are able to isolate patterns in your emotions and behaviors, you can begin to ask yourself where those patterns were born.

4 *Be complicated.* Part of this process is realizing our own complexity. "We're going to ask ourselves

some hard questions, so we've become more self-aware and now we're aware that we're pretty confused." And it's okay!

5 *Values.* As much as you want to become an expert on your inner emotional workings, you want to also keep developing a knowledge of your values. Which is another way of articulating what you care about. The ability to maintain an alignment between you, your values, and your efforts is the secret sauce of productivity. "If you want to run a marathon, you can say, 'It's going to be painful and uncomfortable and it's going to take some time but I made a choice and I want to do it.' As long as you made a choice and you value it, there's nothing wrong with that. But when your values and your behavior aren't in alignment, it's like finding yourself in the middle of a marathon and saying, 'I don't even like running and I don't know how I got here.'"

WHERE ARE YOU AT?

(O for Opportunity)

Opportunity. But not opportunity in the general sense of the word. I'm talking about the reality of women's past, but I also want you to feel the optimism that this word suggests for our and your future. Another way to look at it: personality is who you really are, and opportunity is your specific place in the world as a woman.

In a minute, we'll talk about where you are now. And when I say you, I mean you, dear particular reader, but I also mean you, woman in this culture. In order for women to get what they want out of life, they must understand societal barriers that are in their way and where those come from. In other words, I want to touch on the important roadblocks you/we have faced in the past and the present and the opportunities you/we are poised to capitalize on in the present and beyond. And before you even start with, "I'm not a feminist, I'm for equality for everyone . . ." allow me to stop you. Seriously, stop it.

Let Me Hit You Up with the Facts

+ Women, like people of color, LGBTQ people, and the handicapped, have had fewer opportunities to thrive in our culture than men. It's only due to a consistent effort on the part of feminists (both women and men) that our culture has moved in the direction of equality.

+ After a seventy-year battle for women's suffrage, the Nineteenth Amendment was only ratified in 1920, giving American women the right to vote.

+ And while we've come a long way, baby, remember those tidbits from the beginning of this chapter? American women currently earn just 80 percent of what their male counterparts make. As we move along in our careers, the pay gap only widens rather than narrows.

+ Besides getting paid 20 percent less than men for their efforts, women have to work harder for recognition at work and then head home to put in a few more hours of unpaid work there.

+ Historically (and when I say historically, I'm not talking about that long ago), a woman's worth was tied inextricably to her role as mother and wife. Her whole purpose was to care for her family. Any deviation from this meant you weren't a woman at all. Access to birth control was a game-changing development. Being able to choose when and when not to have children put a powerful tool in women's hands, which is why it was such a hard-won step. It was 1965 before the Supreme Court struck down the last remaining state law that prohibited married couples from accessing birth control. It would be 1972 before those same rights were afforded to single people. These changes in law, and the change to hearts and minds that often follows the law, have been essential for women to move away from the biology-as-destiny role of woman as mother. The power to choose if and when to have children has allowed women the chance to consider other ways to be women in the world.

+ If you remain not quite convinced of the historical importance of feminism and how much we still need it, just take another look at Twitter. Watch what happens to outspoken feminists like Lindy West or Jamilah Lemieux when they tweet about women's rights. The misogyny they face in reaction to their feminism is at best "Girl, relax" and at worst threats of rape and murder.

This list isn't meant to depress you but to remind you that when you face challenges in life, they're frequently supported by historical and political realities that it does no good to ignore. We can't win the game without knowing the rules, and that's a big part of O.

ROADBLOCKS, DETOURS, AND OPEN ROADS

One of the best ways to be able to move forward is to understand what is holding you back. You could be swimming, no holds barred, in optimal health, but if it's against the current, you're just setting yourself up for failure . . . and exhaustion. This self-study and your subsequent findings are crucial to understanding your particular opportunity.

So let's tear it up. What are the realities—good, bad, and ugly—that have an impact on your life? How do we take our knowledge of our own history, our sense of our place in the world now, and turn it into something useful? As much as I wish anything was possible, I'm more interested in getting real about what's possible and desirable *for you.* The whole point of this book is to streamline your efforts so you can move forward rather than just run yourself ragged.

Roadblocks

Of course there are many factors in a person's life that they can't control. Do you dream of rising to the top of your company but the boss's daughter has her eye on the same corner office? Yeah, then not so much for you. If you're a single mom, quitting your job and going back to school full-time to become a lawyer may not be a possibility. Most of us have to make rent or pay a mortgage, and we have family obligations, like kids to care for or parents to help. So there's no point beating yourself up about not being able to muscle your way through those challenges. When you feel yourself coming up against what feels like a roadblock, take a minute to take a closer look. Are you in a situation where there is no way for you to win? Are you forcing yourself to try to accomplish something that you don't really want to? Maybe it's a goal your parents had for you? Maybe it's a job that sounds good on paper but doesn't truly excite you. Sometimes a roadblock is a bitter pill to swallow but sometimes it's an unexpected gift. Realizing you don't really want the thing you thought you wanted means you can free up all that energy to pursue your real goals.

Detours

Detours are different from roadblocks in that there is a way around them. A lack of self-confidence can feel every bit as limiting as the absence of a college degree, but you *can* work on it (and can make progress in much less time than it takes to get through a bachelor's degree). It's hard to change jobs when you're comfortable somewhere, even if that somewhere doesn't recognize your awesomeness.

Open Roads

But for all of those roadblocks, you're likely to see some open roads, too. Your free time really does belong to you. If working out is something you know you need to feel good and de-stress, then it should be on your schedule and that episode on Netflix should come off. Not putting your hand up for every added task at work doesn't mean you're not a team player: it means you're protecting yourself from burnout.

WHAT ARE YOU GOING *TO DO* ABOUT IT?

(P for *Productivity*)

What is productivity anyway? Making the most money you can? Getting the longest list ticked off? The *Oxford English Dictionary* says productivity is "the state or quality of being productive." But it quickly follows up with "the effectiveness of productive effort, especially in industry, as measured in terms of the rate of output per unit of input." At first glance it's a definition that seems to favor the pursuit of more, more, more. And our culture certainly places an emphasis on the grind. But on closer examination—"in terms of the rate of output per unit of input"—it's a reminder that being productive only really sings when the effort you're pouring into your goals pays dividends. It's output *as compared to* units of input.

Your Brain on Busy

There's evidence that killing yourself to crush a longer and more scheduled day is not only *not* going to get you points on the job, it may actually reduce your ability to produce meaningful work. Much research has been done in the field of brain science that looks at what is actually happening in our brains when we're actively engaged in focused activity compared to what happens when we're at rest but awake. We all know (but do not always prioritize) that getting enough sleep is essential to our physical and mental health. Our brains, in particular, require sleep in order to function. It's not only unconsciousness that allows us to operate at high levels, but also waking rest. Throughout the day, we naturally move from stages of being actively engaged with tasks to periods of rest. The latter periods don't have to mean flaking out on the couch—they can mean just looking out a window, daydreaming, allowing your thoughts to drift, or going for a walk without headphones on. All of these resting activities allow the brain to move into what neuroscientists call "default mode network." In this crucial stage, the brain does not take a break, but synthesizes data, almost plays with information, and solves problems. Brain mapping has shown that synapses fire more fluidly when we take a break from work. All of this may explain that "out of the blue" feeling when an idea comes to you in the shower. It may feel like it came out of nowhere, but really your brain was able to go into default mode while you were singing in the shower and find a solution to a problem you weren't able to master while giving it all your attention.

Now, I'm not suggesting you give up concentrated work, but I am saying you cannot get more out of more effort. At least, mostly not. A long-term study done at Florida State University found that most people can only give their full concentration to a task for one hour, and that even the truly gifted—elite athletes, musicians, writers—only work productively for four hours each day. Without downtime and enough sleep, individuals experience incapacitating burnout. These facts apply to both men and women, but when you look at how much less women benefit from doing too much, this science is only more compelling.

Don't Forget About P and O

What are some other ways to look at productivity, then? If we know that looking for praise and recognition from outside sources or chasing goals we don't actually value can be part of a slippery slope to burnout, where else can we turn? How about a chance to decide for ourselves? I'll be asking you to come back to what you'll learn after investigating **P for personality**. Then you'll take into consideration the particular challenges you face as a person and as a woman that you'll be diving into after reading about **O for opportunity**.

Over the course of this book, you'll move toward your own definition of being productive, not just frantically busy. If you're not looking for your mother's pride in your job or your performance review at work to dictate to you your self-esteem, what other clues will you have? Is it a sense of excitement regarding your work? Is it pride in your efforts? What if we decided to narrow our focus down to just the things that made us happy and gave our lives a sense of purpose? One of the hardest steps for many women is to start taking away time and energy from consuming tasks from their lives. Habits are hard to break, particularly if they're habits that make other people happy.

In each chapter that follows, we'll be diving more deeply into the concepts outlined above. We'll walk through the steps necessary to get clear on you and your goals, we'll take away some of the useless crap that's in your way, then we'll supercharge your authentic productivity in ways that will energize you rather than deplete you.

Are you ready? Let's get this shit done.

HERE'S THE DRILL

As you move through this book, I'll be asking you to pause at the end of most chapters and do some work. You'll be defining your goals, looking at what needs to be cleared away in order to reach those goals, and shaping your time so that your schedule supports you rather than breaks you. Whenever you see Here's the Drill, it's time to think about how that chapter speaks to you and works in your life. You may be tempted to skip the exercises and come back and do them after reading the whole book. I urge you to go through the book in order, as each chapter and lesson builds on the last. Many exercises will be quite short, maybe three or four questions for you to make some notes on. Because chapter 1 is where we're establishing who you are in this process, this chapter is the exception. You can either write your answers in this book or, if you'd rather have space to stretch out, you can work in your own notebook or journal.

P

Now shit's going to get real. Since *P* stands for *personality*, we're going to look at who you really are, to create your POP Personality Profile. This isn't supposed to be pretty. We're not talking about your Twitter profile shot—you know, that one of you on your last vacation looking tanned and relaxed, with three filters, obviously. We want warts-and-all honesty about who you are and what you want. Getting real about what drives you is essential to getting what you want out of life. As we've discussed, it's particularly easy for women to be derailed by the needs and desires of those around us, such as family members, mates, and bosses, so it takes conscious effort to zero in on our own desires. Take your time, let your thoughts flow, and write down your answers without judging yourself.

❒ If money were no object, how would you spend your time? In point form, describe an ideal day.

- ❏ What makes you feel proud?

- ❏ What makes you want to go back to bed?

- ❏ What makes you feel jealous?

- ❏ What motivates you? (Money? Recognition?)

- ❏ What makes you want to quit?

- ❏ Do you crave solitude or company at the end of the day?

- ❏ What makes you feel envious?

- ❏ What makes you feel awesome?

- ❏ How did your family life shape you?

- ❏ If you had to choose three words to describe yourself, what would they be?

- ❏ When do you feel healthiest?

- ❏ How often do you compare yourself to others?

- ❏ When do you feel most creative?

- ❏ Whom do you have to please?

- ❏ What drains you?

- ❏ Would you rather lead or follow?

- ❏ What is your best trait?

❏ What is your worst trait?

❏ Do you crave routine or novelty?

❏ What makes you happy?

❏ What makes you unhappy?

Yes, it's a long list! Take your time, make crazy notes, set it aside and come back to it later. Let the questions percolate. Whatever you do, don't be polite with your answers. No one else has to see these notes, so bust out the most honest answers you've got. Once you've really laid it all out there, go back and read your answers. Write a couple of sentences about yourself that sum up where you are now.

For instance:

> I am a person who craves both creativity and structure. I can be envious of the success of others but also thrive in a collaborative environment. I'd like to have my own business, but the thought of other people relying on me makes me want to barf.

or

> I am a person who needs lots of time alone, yet I'm very connected to my friends. I feel proud that people come to me with their problems, and my best trait is that I'm calm under pressure. I'm happiest when I'm in the flow of work and can feel anxious if I can't control my schedule.

or

> I am a person who needs a lot of positive feedback. Know-
> ing other people like me and my work drives me. I'm
> happy when people around me are happy. I don't want to
> try new things if I think I won't succeed.

You're going to keep these sentences—these beliefs in who you are and what you want—in mind as we move along. We'll come back to them as we move through the **POP Effect**.

O

☐ What do the roadblocks, detours, and open roads look like
   in your life. Make some notes about where things lie for
   you in this moment.

For example, do you have a student loan that has to be dealt with? A family member you're responsible for? How much time can you truly call your own to direct as you wish? What's standing in your way? What is in your control and what isn't? Do you have any special advantages, like maybe an inheritance, a job that allows you a lot of flexibility, a well-connected mentor? There's no judgment attached to any of these details—we're just getting the lay of the land.

P

❐ Write a description of your ideal day.

Start from the moment you wake (do you need an alarm?) to when you go to sleep (in 3,000-thread-count sheets!). Do you work, see friends, get outside? Imagine a day with no obligations other than following your interests.

❐ Now look into your own, actual calendar and pick a typical day from the past couple of weeks. Describe that actual day.

CHAPTER TWO

The Only Approval You
Need Is Your Own

Winnipeg, spring 1992: *Get up, stand up*

*O*ne unusually warm spring day in Winnipeg, I hummed quietly to some emo '90s tune that was playing on the radio as I drove to my best friend Joshi's house. As the song ended, a loud ad followed. It announced that there was a competition to find Canada's funniest new comedian and that trials at an open-mic night were happening a couple of weeks later at Yuk Yuk's—a local comedy club. I'm not sure what got into me—although I was a huge stand-up comedy fan, I had never aspired to be a performer before—but by the time I reached Joshi's house I was buzzing with energy and a shiny new project: Joshi and I would team up, write a routine, and compete in that competition. No, *win* that competition.

Understandably, she was a little shocked when I arrived at her doorstep, out of breath with excitement. *A stand-up comedy routine?* Though she hesitated at first, and at second, she knew that look in my eyes all too well. A couple of minutes later we were in her basement, pen and paper in hand, writing down potential ideas.

For the next couple of weeks, we practiced every chance we got—after school, during lunch, on breaks, applying our rigorous studying practices to crude, hopefully funny, sketches. I had never felt so alive.

As the big night approached, we worked at polishing our routine and started to finalize certain details, like, *what would we wear?* Coming from an all-girls school, where we wore uniforms every day of our life, creating the perfect look was an exciting prospect. Sexy, but not too sexy. Likable. Approachable. *Funny?*

So as we entered the club (fake IDs in hand) to compete, we felt pretty good. We had approached this task just like we did our AP chemistry exams—prepare, prepare, prepare! However, nothing we had ever done in life could have prepared us for facing a live, paying crowd who'd come to be entertained and expected to get their money's worth.

There was a big whiteboard with the lineup of the night's amateur acts—and as we got closer and closer to being called, I began to freak out. I watched in horror as very few laughs were granted, more like the odd grunt, and one by one each would-be stumbled from the stage, departing far more deflated than when he'd arrived. I also noticed that both the crowd and the performers were disproportionately male. I looked at my partner, my eyes screaming, *We are waaaay out of our league here,* just as our names were called to go up.

As I reflect on this story—all ten minutes of it—I am reminded of what an incredible microcosm it was, highlighting so many of the things we will talk about in this chapter.

As I walked up onstage, trembling from my core, I was immediately aware that, probably for the first time in any real way, I was being completely observed—*judged*. Judged upon my looks, my stature, my age, my energy. My instinct was to totally retract into myself—to hide. The exact opposite of what needs to happen when you're about to walk onto a stage and perform. The act of being so observed—as an object— made me feel completely vulnerable. I was quick to start scrutinizing my outfit choices, my life choices, and my ability. In the twenty seconds it took to walk up to that stage, my entire sense of self was thrown into chaos.

When we had finally made it up onstage, you could have heard a pin drop. Now, squarely in the aim of a bright spotlight, I faced the dark, faceless, cross-armed crowd. Of course, there are the natural nerves of performing—I had debated in front of hundreds before in national championships, so I knew from nerves—but this was something totally different.

This was an audience, half drunk on flat draft beer, that was thoroughly unimpressed by the sight of two sixteen-year-old girls cowering in front of them. What's more, they could feel the panic wafting off us. They weren't looking at us. They were looking through us. I had never felt so naked in all my life.

So what's the first response in this situation? Not to remember all the work you've put in. Not to rely on your self-worth and dedication. No, my first defense mechanism was *to please*. *To be liked*. Which by its very definition, is the enemy of comedy.

Immediately my voice became diluted. Melting under the heat of that bright light, the only thing you've got is a mic and your voice. We listlessly told our first joke. There wasn't a single reaction, until finally somebody from the back of the crowd screamed, *"We can't hear you!"* Joshi looked at me in a total state of panic, sweat dripping from her brow. I needed our voice to be powerful, not weak—to be confident. I needed to throw their suspicious, penetrating glares off by tossing our words back to them, hoping that through their laughter they would start self-evaluating, instead of crucifying us. I leaned over and whispered to Joshi, signaling a change-up of the order. We had wanted to end on our strongest laugh last, but we needed it now or never. She gulped and nodded, as I said, "Just pretend we're in our uniforms."

A big deep breath. And we began. We delivered our best joke with more gusto than we ever had in practice and, to our great relief, we got a huge, roaring laugh.

We had them. And from that moment on, we didn't let them go. We dug our heels in, relied on all the work we had done, and, in a matter of seconds, instead of seeking approval, adopted a take-it-or-leave-it attitude. It was amazing—the second we gave up caring what they thought, we had their undivided attention.

We bowed after our final joke—to wild applause. Later that night we were announced as the winners. It was only when they were booking our tickets to finals in Toronto that the contest officials were made aware that we were underage—and therefore didn't qualify. But it was beside the point. During that ten-minute set, we learned more about life than we could have in any classroom. I still carry many of these lessons with me today.

POP *Truth:*

WHO'S THE BOSS OF YOU?

Take charge of your life by:

✦ Moving from object to subject.

✦ Ditching busyness.

✦ Learning the sound of your own voice.

"You're not the boss of me!" It's a statement, often accompanied by a stamped foot, that you can expect to hear from a small kid. Children know inherently that the essential struggle of growing up is moving from dependence to autonomy. And while most of us do become independent of those who raised us, we can't always say that we become fully autonomous. Autonomy is defined as freedom from external control or influence. We may never create a world where our own voices are the only ones we listen to (and who would want that?), but where are our voices in the hierarchy of those we listen to?

Who are you listening to in an average day? When you look at your work are you reliving that meeting you had with your boss where she seemed annoyed? When you're getting dressed are you beating yourself up for not getting to the gym more so your skirt fits better? When you think about your partner do you hear your mom questioning when he's going to put a ring on it? It can be really hard to differentiate what you want versus what the rest of the world wants from you, but doing so is vital to moving toward autonomy.

We've already established that being busy for busyness's sake is the road to ruin. Rather, we're blazing a new trail of productivity on our own terms, which means going after the goals that are truly our own. Which means knowing our goals. Which means knowing ourselves. Which means listening to ourselves. Getting comfortable with our own thoughts, feelings, and values and even more comfortable with rejecting the external forces that don't serve us is like tipping the first domino over.

So what stands between us and getting down to the business of doing our thing? Oh, so much.

Historically, there are few groups that haven't taken a run at controlling women. Those who have include the church, government, fathers, husbands, beauty advertisers, the diet industry . . . I could go on. If it weren't so fucking exhausting, it would be flattering. Originally, this control was physical and literal. Women couldn't vote, own property, or manage their own reproductive health. But as laws regarding these things changed, other ways of undermining women's autonomy sprang up and the tools of control have become more emotional and psychological, far more subversive and subliminal. There are many and nefarious ways the world has to encourage you to not listen to yourself. Don't worry, we'll be kicking them all in the teeth shortly, but first we have to understand them.

OBJECT VERSUS SUBJECT

Once an object has been incorporated in a
picture it accepts a new destiny.
—GEORGES BRAQUE

Understanding this concept is crucial to answering one of the very first fundamental questions of **P**—personality—or who are you in your own eyes, as opposed to the eyes of those viewing you. In other words, all the work of trying to understand who you really are (and therefore what you really want) must involve a repositioning of yourself as the subject of each story or scenario as opposed to the object. You're going to be the active player as opposed to the passive.

In my previous story, I moved from subject to object to subject in a matter of minutes—but those switches changed my reality entirely. As I walked up onstage, presumably to entertain and make a roomful of people laugh, I assumed I was the subject. I quickly learned, however, as my confidence melted away in the face of scrutiny and judgment, that I had become the object—something observed (and perhaps ridiculed) for things that were wholly unrelated to my upcoming performance, e.g., my looks, my age, my sex. Until I managed to take my power back in those crucial couple of seconds, I remained observed—and weak. My effect on the audience, despite all my hard work and courage, was bland and faint. Once I decided to start controlling the room (instead of being controlled), I reverted back to the subject of the story, ultimately winning the night and learning a million-dollar lesson.

HOW DO WE BECOME OBJECTS?
LET ME COUNT THE WAYS

So how does this apply to you? Let's take a look at a couple of interesting cultural and historical examples of the ways in which women are pushed toward being objects rather than subjects.

Women may account for more than 50 percent of college enrollment now, but our culture remains dogged in its efforts at placing a woman's value in her attractiveness. You could fill libraries with what has been written on the objectification of women through art, advertising, media, and culture. But a nugget of the phenomenon was boiled down by film theorist Laura Mulvey when she coined the term "the male gaze" in her essay "Visual Pleasure and Narrative Cinema." Mulvey proposed that in classic, Hollywood movies, the camera—and therefore the audience, since the camera is our entrée into the film— assumed a male perspective. That visual vocabulary made the heterosexual male point of view the accepted starting place for images of women. So if we're watching a film and a female character enters the room, she'll be taken in by the camera as if watched by a man, appraised according to his standards as being pleasing or not pleasing. Although Mulvey was using the male gaze in a feminist critique of film, it's easy to find this same lens in use outside of old black-and-white movies. Until recently, in advertising, magazines, and TV, it was exceptional when a male point of view wasn't used when creating female characters.

This expectation that women exist—at least in images if not in reality—for the consumption and pleasure of men is not one that retreated as films moved from black-and-white to glorious Technicolor. It's a badly kept, if vomit-inducing, secret that actresses must pass the "do I want to fuck her" test among certain Hollywood executives to get cast in leading roles. Amy Schumer satirized this cliché in her scorchingly funny short "Last Fuckable Day." Schumer plays herself, out for a hike when she comes across Tina Fey and Patricia Arquette at an abundantly set table, toasting Julia Louis-Dreyfus on finally reaching her last fuckable day as an actress. When Schumer is in disbelief that a woman as beautiful as Louis-Dreyfus could be considered past her best-before date, Louis-Dreyfus shrugs. "Nobody was more shocked than me that I was allowed to be fuckable through my forties and into my fifties . . . I thought *Us Weekly* had made some kind of clerical error."

While many women writers and directors are actively reclaiming ownership of female imagery, it remains that they need reclaiming because the assumption is that female imagery has belonged to men. And the prevalence of these kinds of images has normalized the straight-guy POV so much that it's not just men who take on these values but women, too. Across the culture, we're encouraged to believe that women are here to be observed rather than to be observers, to be objects rather than subjects. We internalize this message into our own thoughts and feelings. Women are so highly sensitive to the experience of being observed that we do something psychologists call "habitual body monitoring." This is the experience of thinking about your own body and how it looks to others, and many women do it as often as *once per minute.* You could be sitting in a meeting and think, *How do my legs look the way I'm sitting? Do my arms look flabby when I cross them this way? Is that person noticing my gray hair?* Not surprisingly, habitual body monitoring is closely associated with feelings of dissatisfaction. In other words, we're not saying to ourselves, "Man, I look fine in this meeting!" That any mental and emotional bandwidth is being taken up with thoughts of how your body appears to others is at minimum a distraction and at worst a form of self-torture. The bottom line is, when you're thinking these thoughts, you're taking up space that could be used to get relevant shit done.

Another way that our well-developed abilities for self-objectification can play out is in the bedroom. Many women find it difficult to be in the moment while being intimate. Rather, they do something that Masters & Johnson named "spectatoring," which is kind of floating above yourself and your partner and observing what's going on, rather than being present. Again, this isn't a positive. Women who do this are critiquing their own bodies or second-guessing whether they're pleasing their partners. Just as in the workplace, this objectifying is taking you out of the moment and into the periphery of experience, which is a far more diluted, less effective place to be.

A study out of Royal Holloway, University of London, found that women with a tendency to self-objectify (that is, to value their appearance over their competence) were less able to feel their own pulse (a standard body-awareness task used by scientists). Researchers couldn't establish whether these women were less sensitive to their own bodies as a result of objectifying themselves or whether being less in tune with their bodies led to them seeing themselves as objects. Whatever the answer to this chicken-or-egg question, it's clear that a disconnect between ourselves and our bodies has a powerful impact on women.

These invisible habits may not seem directly related to productivity, but that's just how sneaky patriarchy is. The relationship between self-objectifying and sexual dysfunction and disordered eating is well documented. But these cultural forces, and the depressing habits that result from them, impact us in more pedestrian ways, too. On a basic level they have us listening to others rather than to ourselves. A lot of mental space and energy go into worrying about how we look to others and how well we meet preexisting expectations. Women have been watched, judged, and examined, and as a result we have worked and behaved to please others instead of ourselves. When we measure our worth according to outside expectations, is it any wonder we're constantly trying to do so much? If we're not keeping everyone around us happy, we feel that we're not enough.

Moving from object to subject is an essential step in becoming autonomous, identifying your goals, and moving toward them. In order to take control of your life, happiness, and productivity, you also have to no longer react to how others perceive you. Essentially, you have to be your badass self and not give a shit if you piss off a few people in the process. Instead, you have to learn to actively create (and validate) your own image and your own life path.

Okay, easier said than done, I grant you that.

A Few Ideas for Practicing Doing Rather Than Being

1 *Move.* When you move your body—run, hike, dance, swim—think about the wonder that it is. Focusing on your body's abilities rather than its attractiveness can help shift your feelings.

2 *Watch your judgments of other women.* If you find yourself raising an eyebrow about another woman's "slutty" outfit, realize you're doing the culture's policing job for it.

3 *Take note of double standards around you.* Female bodies are more often on display—and up for discussion—in TV, movies, and music videos, than men's bodies.

4 *Ease up on consuming "who wore it better" media.* Critiquing celebs based on their bodies and their looks is almost always aimed at women, not men.

5 *Give yourself a break.* When you catch yourself body monitoring, take note and try to let it go. Bring your focus back to what you're doing rather than how you're looking.

THE BUSYNESS TRAP

Beware of the barrenness of a busy life.

—SOCRATES

Have you ever asked a woman how she is and had her answer any way other than, "So busy!"? And I don't think it's bragging. I think when you add up work, unpaid domestic work, and emotional labor, we're busy. And we know that being in fifth gear all day is likely to result in emotional and physical burnout. But what has it got to do with productivity and self-direction? Isn't being busy the way to get things done? The short answer is no. For those addicted to striking items off their to-do lists, this is hard information to take in. How can it be possible to be productive without being busy? The radical leap I'm asking you to make demands you do exactly that: be more productive by being less busy.

The reality is that the very structure of our days—in which we rush from task to task, cramming in as much as we can—not only reduces our ability to be creative, it also takes away our ability to know our own minds. When we are engaged in focused work, working without pause through that to-do list, we are using our left brain. Remember our little brain-science chat from chapter 1? We also need quiet, meditative time (remember default network mode?) for our right brain to process information and come up with creative solutions, but also to make value-based choices. In other words, we need less activity and more calm so that we can literally know our own opinions.

When we're moving at breakneck speed, making it hard for ourselves to check in with our actual desires and opinions, that void is more easily filled by others. If you're not sure what you think or of what you feel, it's much easier for someone else to tell you what you should think and feel. And as we've talked about earlier, the world is only too happy to tell women stories that hold them back in a myriad of ways.

I recently read a fascinating account of what happens to the brain in the face of all this busyness. According to Iain McGilchrist, the psychiatrist and author of *The Master and His Emissary: The Divided Brain and the Making of the Western World*, the brain is divided into two hemispheres: the right brain (creativity/the Master) and the left brain (reason/the emissary). And though it is a complex scientific evaluation, the gist goes something like this: All creativity comes from the right brain. All effort and action come from the left brain. The more action the left brain takes, the more stifled the creativity of the right brain. The calmer the left brain is, the more the right brain/creativity flourishes. While both sides of our brain, along with their capacities, are essential, McGilchrist makes the point that as a culture, we have come to value the left brain over the right brain.

Bringing back balance by favoring the right brain and creativity is especially important to women, in my opinion. Creativity represents everybody's true voice: it's what makes every individual unique. Whether you're an actual artist or just someone who needs to solve problems as part of your job, creativity is essential. The more we're doing just to do—*the more we're doing just to check things off a list*—the more difficult it is to hear that creative voice and to know who we really are, and what we want and need. This is why an analysis of our own personal busyness is a must if we're ever to start putting emphasis, effort, and energy into the things that really represent who we are and what we want, so true productivity can be achieved.

In chapter 6, we'll take a closer look at how to get an accurate snapshot of how your time is spent.

VOICES IN MY HEAD

Either you must control your thoughts or the outside forces will control them and be warned that the outside forces are usually negative.
—MADDY MALHOTRA

Moments before I walked into that dark, seedy comedy club, my head was full of positive thoughts and empowering messages about what I had achieved, even before stepping onstage. I knew I had done the work and was thrilled to have discovered a new part of myself in the process. As soon as I was in the throes of uncertainty and a free-falling confidence (a rare case for me, but for many this is a daily, albeit less dramatic occurrence), it was amazing the warp speed at which positivity all but disappeared. Not only was my reassuring voice gone, it was replaced by the voice of anyone who had ever told me I couldn't do something, and the paranoid delusions of what I thought the audience was thinking of me. Rapidly, my thoughts switched from substantive reinforcement about the work I had done to cheap insecurities about my looks, my personality, and my abilities. It was only when I was able to force those voices out of my head and replace them with my own that things started to turn around.

Whose are the voices you hear when you're unsure? Sadly, it's easiest to home in on the negative ones from our past. When you're feeling unhappy with your body, do you mentally and emotionally flash back to that ballet instructor who snapped at you to suck in your gut? Does being nervous before making a presentation at work put you in your eight-year-old shoes, when your teacher said public speaking would never be your thing? Even if the feedback you received was positive and encouraging, it might make finding your own opinions a challenge.

When I look back on my own perfectionist tendencies in childhood, I feel like I was born with them. But can that really be right? If I think back to early conversations with my parents, I got a lot of attention from them when I brought home As. Now of course, what parent doesn't praise a good report card? But something in me became awfully addicted to the endorphin rush that came along with pleasing. Deciding to not go to law school was a surprisingly easy call to make. I knew it was the wrong path for me and I didn't want to go. But sitting at that brunch table telling my parents? That was a killer. I hated letting them down, and making a choice that I thought they wouldn't be cheering on took every ounce of strength I had. What's even more bizarre about this is that after their initial shock, my parents actually *did* cheer me on (just like they had initially in Toronto). I was just projecting my own fears onto what I *thought* their reaction would be. Now this is getting into some pretty wacko psychoanalytic stuff that I'm certainly not qualified to break down, but the point is, the scared, unsure, unconfident mind is a pretty crazy place filled with doubt and guilt. I still don't love doing things my parents disapprove of. I trust their judgment and look for their input on big decisions. But I've learned through practice to distinguish between my impulse to agree with them and what my own opinions are.

These are tough lessons, even for someone who says she seemed to be born knowing her own mind. My friend and fellow wellness blogger Lori Deschene is the creator of the popular site *Tiny Buddha*. She tells me she was the kind of kid who defiantly chose a dinosaur when other girls were reaching for Barbies at the toy store. "I've always felt like it was my identity to go against the grain. I've always seen myself as a rebel, a risk taker, a dreamer." In fact, she says, she has had to check to make sure that she's not making choices just to be contrary. "I had to learn that sometimes what I want truly is what other people are doing."

But what about when you find yourself definitively on the outside of a mainstream choice? Knowing your own values doesn't make it any less uncomfortable when the people you love don't love the decisions you're making. About four years ago Lori and her boyfriend got engaged. They shared the happy news with family and friends. Except, shortly after, they admitted to each other that neither of them actually wanted to be married *at that point in their lives*. They knew they could change their minds in time, if, for example, they had children. But at this point they were in love, they were committed, and that felt like enough, even if all their friends were getting married. In the face of the pressure our culture puts on couples to go down the seemingly inevitable road to matrimony, Lori and her boyfriend had to be honest that they wanted to make a different choice. And then they had to let everyone know there was to be no wedding. "We got a lot of flak for going back on that decision. Because we were engaged. There were people who were surprised and disappointed. And it was very uncomfortable for both of us, because whenever it would come up, people would say, 'When are you getting married?' For a while I still called him my fiancé and that would inevitably bring up the question. Now I just say 'my boyfriend,' because we're not planning to get married anytime soon."

Deciding to marry or not is clearly too significant a decision to allow outside forces to take charge of it. And yet . . . cultural norms coupled with the desire to please one's family make opting out painfully difficult. It can be difficult even if the decision isn't so momentous. Lori says, "If I had to give some advice, it's finding that sweet spot between not just trying to be different, and also not going with the flow just for the sake of fitting in." Identifying where you are on the spectrum between fitting in and going your own way is the first step. And Lori leaves me with this gem: "The only question that I think is important to ask ourselves is, 'What would I do if I knew no one would judge me?'"

When you're about to make any big decision or take major action, the first voices you often hear in your head are the answers to "What will he think?" or "Will she think I'm making a mistake?" These voices and opinions and the hypothetical responses from others often become so loud that they drown out your own. As a result, you're often left with a lot of ambivalence and uncertainty. For women, raised to be acutely in touch with the feelings and desires of others, ambivalence can feel like a central part of our characters. Our strength—our empathy, our ability to acknowledge other perspectives—can also be our weakness. The psychiatrist Anita Chakrabarti describes it like this: "The confusion can come from being aware of all these different perspectives. Instead of making a choice, and saying, 'This is the thing I'm going to do, I know it's not perfect but this is the thing I choose to work on,' we're answering to all these different perspectives. We want to make the right choice so we keep distracting ourselves, saying, 'That's right, no, this is right, no, that's right, too,' and we can get lost in it."

Once you've identified the voices and pressures you want out of your head, it's time to cultivate the one you do want: yours. But first you've got to hear it. Thanks to underuse, it may be barely a whisper. And so, how best to shake off this can't-see-the-forest-for-the-trees feeling of taking in everyone's real or perceived opinions about our choices? According to Anita, "This is where mindfulness is really helpful, because mindfulness is doing one thing in the moment, nonjudgmentally."

I've seen this process in action in other women, too. Sam Negrin, who worked with me at LEAF, is a creative person with a lot of confidence in her life choices. But even Sam, someone who has always followed her own path, was recently put off course. Temporarily.

"The way I've always dealt with things is to talk to people. I'll share my ideas. But recently I've been working on a new project and it's kind of big. It has been the biggest struggle because it's a life- and career-changing move. I'll talk to my friends about it, and I had one friend say, 'Who do you think you are, thinking you can do this?' This is someone that is not much of a friend anymore. But I had that feedback of 'Why do you think you can do this and be successful at it, you're going to fail, you're going to fall on your face.' But then on the other hand, I've had, 'Yes, that's an amazing idea, go for it, you can do whatever you want to do!'" After hearing such polarizing reactions, Sam was rattled. "I've had to take a major step back in talking about this with a lot of people. Because I started to get influenced negatively. And I was like, 'Oh, my God, what am I doing?'"

All the negative comments and even some of the kinder but still cautionary remarks took a toll on Sam's plan. She stopped working on her project for two months, but she also took a break from inviting other people's feedback. She slowly started to focus on her own thoughts and desires again. For several weeks, she'd spend some time every day writing down her thoughts, her plans, and her goals, and doing so brought her right back to where she had started. She loved her idea and, moreover, was putting the plan in place to see it through. "When I stopped talking to people and I just listened to myself and I let everything marinate for a couple of weeks, I was like, 'You know, this is a good idea and I'm going to pursue it.' It might not work out. But I think something a lot of people don't realize is that when you want something, it will probably work out in a way you didn't originally think it would."

And being okay with that shift between what a goal looked like in your imagination and what it becomes in reality means you're staying present through the process. Jaclyn Johnson of the successful Create & Cultivate conferences told me about her own shifting expectations. When she first launched her business and was only breaking even, she thought she'd failed. Her parents, both business owners, reminded her that for a start-up, breaking even is a win. It gave Jaclyn an important lesson in perspective. "What you really have to do when you're in it is define your own success, see your own success metric."

START WITH OHM

The little things? The little moments? They aren't little.
—JON KABAT-ZINN

One of the most powerful tools available to women in search of clarity of direction and increased, meaningful productivity is mindfulness. It's a trendy buzzword right now, but it's simply the practice of nonjudgmental, present-moment awareness. Because people confuse it with meditation, it feels like something you've got to schedule, like your Pilates class, but in fact it's something you can use anytime, anywhere. The practice of mindfulness allows us to slow down, stop being so reactive, quiet down the chatter of the world and our own thoughts, and make better decisions.

Now, you may be thinking, *I thought this book was about produc-*

tivity—*and now we're talking about mindfulness?!* What's the correlation? Being mindful, while it may evoke images of ashrams and flowing yogi robes, is actually a key ingredient to supercharging productivity. If you are able to cut through the constant chatter in your head, to silence the outside voices and *their agendas*, if you are able to assess every situation from a point of clarity about who you are and what you want, then you are able to much more quickly clear the path not only to getting more done (through decisive, confident action) but, more important, to getting the *right* stuff done. You'll spend more time on the stuff that moves your fulfillment agenda forward, and less time on the stuff that doesn't.

So here is the vicious circle: without mindfulness, we're at the mercy of our own bitchy inner critic, as well as the actual bitchy critics of the world, both urging us to work harder, faster; but to create mindfulness takes practice, and who's got time for that?

From now on, *you do*. Okay, before you get mad at me for adding one more thing to your to-do list, hang on. This isn't another meeting to add to your calendar, it's a life-changing ninja move that's going to make everything you do better. And of course it's going to put you in closer touch with your own beliefs and opinions.

This is the core mind-set shift that thousands of self-empowerment articles boil down to: to change your life, you must remain present in your life. You must shush that nagging internal critic, stop your ears to the pressures of sexism, and silence the siren call of numbing tactics (whether it's mindless eating, drinking, TV watching, posting on Instagram, or anything else that you may be using to escape reality or look for affirmation). This is the first step to taking your internal and external worlds into your own hands and being totally present with each moment, rather than frustrated, disappointed, and divided.

SO HOW DO I DO IT?

Mindfulness is simply the practice of being in the current moment. Often, we're in about five different places at once, aren't we? You're in a meeting at work, but you're also rehashing an edgy conversation you had that morning with your boyfriend, you're reading into the frown on your boss's face, you're anticipating how your argumentative colleague is going to respond to your ideas . . . And it's very loud inside your head! Mindfulness means existing in the moment you're in rather than doing that mental and emotional multitasking that distracts us.

When you start practicing mindfulness, it may be helpful to actually stop what you're doing, find a quiet spot, and actually focus on your breathing. Even if you just do this for a minute, it will bring your focus back to yourself and help quiet your own busy mind. The Buddhist monk Thich Nhat Hanh teaches a quick and simple habit: "The exercise is simply to identify the in-breath as in-breath and the out-breath as out-breath. When you breathe in, you know that this is your in-breath. When you breathe out, you are mindful that this is your out-breath." By identifying your breaths as they come in and out of your body, you give your mind a simple focus. "When you do that, the mental discourse will stop. You don't think anymore. You don't have to make an effort to stop your thinking; you bring your attention to your in-breath and the mental discourse just stops. That is the miracle of the practice."

If you've never done it before, you may feel silly or fidgety at first. That's okay. To begin, find two times in your day when you can focus on your breath for one minute. Maybe you do it first thing in the morning, before you're even out of bed, and maybe you do it again on the commute home. What feels weird at first will soon become a comfortable habit you can use at will.

Once your body and mind know the feeling of letting go of distraction and coming back home to themselves, you'll be able to drop into mindfulness more often and without silence and solitude. A trick some proponents of mindfulness use is to tell yourself what you're doing. It's a gentle way of bringing your own focus back into the moment and letting go of thoughts and feelings from the past or future that may distract you. It's almost like you're narrating your actions. You can think, *I'm eating lunch*, bringing you into mindfulness (rather than mindlessly eating), or *I'm deciding what to do next* (rather than allowing your mind to race to the opinions of others).

Far from being flaky, mindfulness is a tool for sharp thinking, clear decision-making, and greater productivity. You're able to make decisions because you're clearing your mind from distraction, but you're also able to make the right decision for you because you're listening to your own voice.

Working through all the shifts we're talking about in this chapter requires you to make one essential decision: *that you're worth the effort.* Therapists often describe patients' inability to see the difference between self-interest and selfishness. Particularly for women, putting effort into you and your thoughts, goals, and desires can feel wrong. But it's important to accept that knowing yourself is not the same as putting yourself and your interests above everyone else. It can take time and practice to get comfortable with putting your needs at the top of your own list. And making yourself a priority doesn't make you an unkind person. As Brené Brown says, *compassion requires boundaries.*

In order to take control of your life, happiness, and productivity, you have to shift your focus away from others and how they perceive you, to your own judgment. Essentially, you have to be your own champion and not give a shit if you piss off a few people in the process. Breaking the habit of constantly looking for approval or a reaction is difficult to do in this instant-gratification society, but it's essential to help you transition into the driver's seat of your own life.

Here's the Drill

- ❐ Name a time when you haven't acted on something because you were afraid of what people would think.

- ❐ How did you feel giving up on that idea?

- ❐ Name a time when you did act on something, regardless of (or in the face of) scrutiny. How did it turn out? How did you feel accomplishing it?

- ❐ Whose judgment do you look to most often?

- ❐ Name a time when you had to make a big presentation or big announcement and your thoughts were more firmly on how you looked or what people would think, instead of focused on the actual presentation.

- ❐ What did that do to your confidence?

- ❐ Are you able to remain calm, focused, and objective when difficult situations arise at work or at home?

- ❐ In these situations, does your mind race to find fault with yourself?

❏ After analyzing your answers to these questions, write down three of your strongest traits.

❏ Then write down three of your most original traits (these may cross over with the above).

When faced with a challenge, problem, or difficult situation at work or at home—even if it's a small thing—I want you to recite these six traits to yourself and say which of these you are going to rely on now to solve this problem. For example, "In this talk I will be articulate and compelling. In this talk I will be collaborative and warm. In this talk I will be determined and funny." Be enthusiastic with yourself. Don't allow time for doubt, and then distraction, to seep in.

CHAPTER THREE

You and Your Smart Mouth

Winnipeg, winter 1992: *Death by yes*

*O*ne of my earliest experiences in death-by-yes happened in my last couple of years of high school. And yet, I only realized it a handful of years ago, when I was buried in another like situation. At the beginning of grade eleven, I began to gear up for the university application marathon. I had only two schools on my list: Harvard and Columbia. There was no question in my mind that I would go to one of these two schools (though I did have a backup, McGill). So I began to create my two-year trophy-collecting agenda. I was already, of course, class president, but that was just the beginning. Over the course of the next eighteen months there was nothing I didn't say yes to. And I mean nothing. If it looked good on my application, I did it. I took every AP class I could. I was captain of the debate team, chair for the international debate championships to be held at my school, and chair of the school dance committee. I ran the school canteen (creating the first student-paying job at my school), which meant that on any break, during lunchtime, or after school I was peddling Doritos and ice cream sandwiches to ravenous fellow students. I needed to do this like I needed a hole in the head. On weekends, I was a volunteer candy striper at the hospital. Then I ran for and won head girl (as a result of the most detailed, planned-out, and longest self-imposed campaign ever, I won with the highest margin of victory ever seen at Balmoral) and later went on to become valedictorian, all while maintaining a straight 4.0. And these were just the major things I did. Are you getting the picture? So as I careened into the final applications process, with a couple of interviews at both my top choices, I was feeling pretty bloody confident. How could they *not* let me in? My only competition was a foreign exchange student from Thailand who had come to my school in grade eleven. She had impressive grades and an incredible work ethic but, unlike me, she had only one extracurricular activity: she'd created and ran the new Winnipeg branch of the International Red Cross. True, she spent a lot of time on it—and did an amazing job—but that was only *one* thing!

So you can imagine my shock and horror as I stood at the mailbox reading letters from both universities telling me I had only been *waitlisted*. This horror seemed like a cakewalk, however, compared to the following morning's news: that my rival had been accepted to both.

I could not understand how this had happened. I truly felt that I had been robbed. There was literally *nothing else* I could have done. Time would not have permitted it. And now, the course of my life, as I had planned it, had been irrevocably changed. I felt powerless. Eventually, I summoned the strength to pack my bags and attend McGill—an experience I wouldn't change for anything. But the haunting conundrum of this failure spun over and over in my head for the next twenty years. There was a faint uncertainty in every action I took after that. It wasn't the outcome that paralyzed me—it was that I had been so certain that my process was correct, and yet it had failed me, and I had no idea why.

It was with great relief, then, that one day a couple of years ago, as I was coaching a blogger for *Pick the Brain*, I stumbled upon an epiphany. This blogger was very bright and successful, but she was constantly exhausted and energy-depleted. When I asked her what a typical week looked like for her, she rattled off a never-ending list. I was tired just reading it! Her problem was obvious: she was doing too much. "Power comes from simplicity," I remember telling her, and as the words rolled out of my mouth a light bulb went off. I immediately flashed back to the mailbox twenty years ago. I got it. *Finally*. For every yes that was unnecessary, for every committee that was unnecessary, for any effort toward something that didn't truly represent my real value proposition, I had depleted my offering. I had depleted myself. And the person who had stripped back to her core strength had triumphed. A huge weight lifted. I began to reassess my current life to start reviewing all the times I was saying yes when I could be saying no.

Now this might seem like a trivial example—*what a crisis, you only got into McGill*—but the lesson is this: while I was busy saying yes, I had narrowed my options and my choices. At that time, they were the biggest, most meaningful choices of my life. Your power comes from the choices you make. And again, I wouldn't change my experience at McGill for anything in the world—but I recognize how lucky I was that my default turned out to be so good for me. Now, when I find myself hesitating to say yes to something, I remember this time in my life and the way I felt.

POP *Truth:*

LANGUAGE SHAPES US.

Three words to immediately reevaluate:

- ✦ Start saying **no**.

- ✦ Stop saying, I'm **sorry**.

- ✦ Release the crippling noose of **should**.

I am a writer, so words matter to me. I make a living from them. But for someone who places great value on their importance (I often spend many minutes on just one word choice), it was staggering to realize how careless I was with my everyday speech. Why would I take so much care and act with such precision when communicating what my *fictional characters* felt and desired and yet be so cavalier with things that represent my needs and wants? Clear, direct communication is a foundation of success and part of its fulfillment. Being able to articulate what you want, what your abilities and responsibilities are and *who you are*, is the bedrock of getting things done effectively.

How many times have you agreed to something but as the words are coming out of your mouth, you're already regretting them?

How many times have you apologized for your own behavior, when there is absolutely nothing to apologize for?

How often do you drop what you'd like to be doing in favor of what you think you should be doing?

If you're anything like I was, the answer to these questions is: daily. If I wasn't squeezing in an after-work networking event every night, I was busy apologizing to a friend that I couldn't hang out on the weekend. It was always something. And while there are immediate consequences to this behavior—a constant state of low-level discomfort—it's the long-term consequences that are far more troublesome. I want to underscore the power of *saying what you mean*. In this phase of the POP System, you're clarifying who you are and what you want; the language you use in the world and in your own head is an essential component of that. It is fundamental to personal power. The converse is also true—not saying what you mean will inevitably weaken you. And every time you do it, it chips away at your personal power, without exception. It dissolves your self-confidence. It silences your true voice. And as a result, it is impossible to get things done in a meaningful way. How could it be otherwise? You can't move forward effectively if you aren't operating as a whole version of yourself.

In our path to unleashing your most authentic, kick-ass self, I'm going to take something away from your vocabulary, but then I'm going to give you something back. Sound fair? This linguistic swap may seem small, but I promise you, it's going to pay huge dividends. The truth is, all words matter—but small tweaks are very powerful and a great place to start.

NO MEANS NO

Don't say yes when you really mean no.
—PAULO COELHO

Let's start with what I want to add to your daily dialogue (both external and internal)—IMO, one of the most powerful words in the English dictionary is *no*. It's such a tiny little word. It takes up so little space on the page, it hardly seems worth mentioning. But in life, it's a power source of superhero proportions. *No* is your cape, your Wonder Woman bracelets, your ultimate superpower. Like all superpowers, you'll have to understand it, develop it, and learn to wield it with confidence.

WHY DO WE DO IT?

At the center of your being you have the answer; you
know who you are and you know what you want.
—LAO TZU

Traditional thinking goes that to get ahead you must say yes to every opportunity that comes your way. And if what is coming your way is a door swinging open, leading you toward *your* true goals, then hell yes you're saying yes. If you dream of setting up shop as a florist, you only need your own permission (and a sense of your own value) to say yes to creating arrangements for your first wedding party. A spot opens up in a seminar featuring a leader in your field and I'm packing your bags for you while you're saying yes. When your partner—who is a true partner in fun, shared responsibility, as well as love—wants to take things to the next level and move in together, then yes, yes, yes!

What yes shouldn't be is a blank check, and for many of us it is. Having been raised to be agreeable, helpful, nice girls, women are prone to say yes to things without considering how it affects them. We've been trained so thoroughly to help others that it feels good to do it, as it reinforces a positive sense of self we were brought up to have. I bet just reading these sentences is setting off alarm bells. *Is Erin telling me to stop thinking of others? Is she actually encouraging me to be selfish? Who will like me if I put myself first?* Let me be clear: of course there's nothing wrong with helping others. But the fact that asking you to think of all you do for others without first considering yourself feels uncomfortable shows you how the helpful/selfish binary is set up in a way that's profoundly unhelpful to women.

Let's just break down how yes often works in a woman's life.

Yes Scenario #1

You're in a meeting at work and there are, say, eight or nine people around the table, men and women. Your boss needs someone to take minutes, type them up, and then distribute them after the meeting. "Katie, do you mind jotting down some notes?" Of course Katie will! She's awesome. And helpful. And wants to please her boss, whom she'll be meeting with soon about her performance review. No bigs. But it means that Katie is not really participating in the meeting now. She'd walked into the meeting with a plan to pitch a few ideas for an upcoming project. But it's hard to articulate those ideas while she's taking notes. After the meeting, Katie heads back to her desk, and instead of diving back into her work, she spends forty-five minutes typing up the minutes and emailing them to the group.

Yes Scenario #2

Tight deadlines mean everyone is working late at Julia's office. They'll likely be working until at least 9 p.m. tonight. As he gathers the staff to let them know it's going to be a long night, Julia's manager turns to her and says, "Do you mind putting together the dinner order?" To be honest, she'd rather get on with the revisions that will get their work done sooner, but what is she going to do, say no in front of the whole team? So instead she says, "Sure." Which is another form of yes. Julia then spends no less than thirty minutes going from cubicle to cubicle, taking everyone's dinner order, hunting down the office corporate card, calling in the order, and then running down to the lobby to pick up the food once it arrives.

Yes Scenario #3

Every six months at Jane's accounting firm, a new set of students appear and have to be oriented to office procedures and, let's be honest, babysat for the first few days. Strictly speaking, it's an HR job, but since they really know the job best, the task usually falls to one of the accountants. For the last three seasons, Jane's boss has asked her if she can "keep an eye on the new students." It can be fun to work with the eager newcomers, but to be real, it means that about once an hour someone is at her desk needing direction regarding the software systems, where files are kept, how the company likes things done, etc.

————————

These are just three classic "housekeeping" tasks that are frequently delegated to women in workplaces. There are many, many more small tasks that make office life better. And is it any wonder? It's nice when somebody brings cupcakes in for a going-away party. It's great when someone takes the time to clean out the disgusting office fridge. It's really sweet when someone gets a birthday card and passes it around for everyone to sign. It's these gestures and efforts that make a workplace run smoothly and even feel like a good place to be every day. Somebody needs to do them, and that somebody usually has a vagina. But make no mistake, these tasks, while essential, do not forward a career. Your boss may appreciate that you're a great team player and love the way you're willing to pitch in on these minor jobs, but they won't be moving the needle when it comes time for your performance review.

The social science researcher Madeleine Heil calls performing these jobs "altruistic citizenship behavior." For women to be considered good citizens in the workplace, they must attend to these housekeeping tasks. But don't imagine you're getting bonus points for taking minutes, making coffee, or planning birthday lunches—these duties are just the minimum requirement for women. While these jobs don't bring us glory at work, not doing them can have consequences. Women are expected to be helpful. Men are expected to be ambitious. In a 2005 study of college students, Heil looked at how we perceive women and men when it comes to these citizenship behaviors. The study looked at men and women who helped and didn't help and at how each group was then perceived. Heil found that women who were helpful and got on board with the housekeeping tasks of the workplace were not considered notable or praiseworthy, but simply as doing what women should be doing. Men, on the other hand, achieve rock star status if they engage in housekeeping tasks, because no one expects them to do it in the first place. If women do not meet gender expectations, they are judged more harshly by men and women alike. Men do not meet the same kind of censure when they sidestep helping out.

Just to sum up: women are asked and expected to do more of the administrative tasks (that are not in their job descriptions) that make office life hum, and we're expected to handle the niceties that make workplaces pleasant, but we benefit from neither. When women help in the workplace, they don't benefit; when they don't help in the workplace, they are penalized. When men don't help, no one notices, and when they do help, men benefit from their efforts.

If the unspoken drag of sexism has its way with us at work, what about at home? We know that after a day of work, women put in more hours maintaining their homes and caring for their families. But on top of cooking, loading the dishwasher, doing laundry, overseeing homework, etc., there's another kind of housekeeping that women are expected to attend to. Emotional labor is another item women add to their to-do list, without even considering another option.

Think you're not familiar with emotional labor? Sure you are! Remembering which of your kid's friends have allergies, sending family Christmas cards, booking the sitter, organizing dinners out with friends, knowing everyone's schedule, deciding what's for dinner, researching vacation plans, knowing where things are located at home . . . This is the nearly invisible work that women do at home.

I asked Leah McLaren how this plays out in her home. She's an in-demand writer with books and screenplays, and has a high-profile byline to her name. Her husband also has a big job, which, unlike her, he does at an office. They have three young sons and the complicated schedules that come with modern family life. She's written about the emotional labor that women put into their relationships and can cite research into the origins of this phenomenon and how it puts women at an unfair disadvantage in terms of resources. But what she's not quite able to do is remove it from her own marriage. As Christmas approached last year, she went ahead and looked after all the gifts she and her husband would give their sons, her family, and his. Now, this wasn't a chore she shouldered after a conversation like, "I'll look after gifts if you're good with planning the dinner we're hosting." She didn't consider another option before taking it on. Shortly before the holiday, the issue did get raised. "Rob said, 'Is that all looked after?' And I said, 'Yeah.' And that was our whole conversation about Christmas gifts."

Years of saying yes to every opportunity that came her way was part of how the Canadian talk show host Tracy Moore felt she had to operate. "I was absolutely a 'yes' person. And I always felt like I *can* do this. It's humanly possible for me to do it, therefore I should do it. I should just say yes. I should just fit it in." As a high-profile personality—her gorgeous smile and warm wit are beamed into homes across the country every day—Moore is in demand. She's asked to appear at events, represent products, speak to groups, and the list goes on. "There was a moment I remember paying out of pocket to volunteer. So I was paying for a cab all the way to the West End, in a snowstorm, and getting there and feeling like there's absolutely nothing that can happen here that will ever make me feel appreciated for this role, this drive that I just took, and this money that I just spent, and that's wrong. That is not the essence of volunteering. Volunteering should be something you do because it makes you feel good and where it feels right to give. Whereas all I was feeling was resentful. So that was a moment where I thought, *I've got to re-jig the way I am doing things.* Because I'm doing things just to do them, and my heart is not in it."

All that saying yes had her feeling ragged and out of control. "What

I came to realize is that when I say yes all the time, the people that pay the price are usually my family, mostly my husband. I'm mean to my husband when I'm overscheduled. I just am. He used to pay the price by being the parent that picks up all the pieces. I'm short with my kids. And I feel like they're getting in the way, when really they *are* the way. They are the ones. I realized over time that the yes was not really taking me to a good place, so I started to really drastically scale back on the yeses."

Switching from a jam-packed schedule to one that is carefully considered and dramatically pared down wasn't an easy change. Rather than experiencing relief, initially she felt like a failure. She'd ask herself why she couldn't do it all. "Whereas now the feeling of saying no is very empowering. I feel like I have options, I'm allowing myself to see things in terms of a choice now rather than just, 'Yeah, I'll throw myself into it.'"

Starting to decline offers can feel like a gamble. What if no one ever asks again? What if that gig—even though it wasn't really interesting to you and even though it didn't pay much money, or any money—was the last to come along? It takes a kind of confidence as well as a leap of faith to put your time into going after what you want rather than taking what comes along. And although she used to worry about letting people down, Moore quickly found the response to her new attitude was almost always positive. "People see that I'm willing to say no and it ups my value. And I'm really okay to go without what they're offering. Therefore, they think, *We have to offer her more or make it a better deal for her.*"

Not everyone's phone is blowing up with offers and invitations like Moore's, but even at the beginning of a career it's still possible to be intentional with your choices. And even in those crappy situations where you don't really have a choice, it's an important mental exercise to think of what you want, what you'd do if you had choices, since as your career and life develop you *will* have more choices.

When and How to Say No

+ Get honest with yourself about what you want to do and what you don't want to do but continue doing because you don't want to disappoint anyone.

+ Point out the problem. If you're in a workplace where you feel you're doing too much housekeeping and not enough of your actual job, let your manager know. Of course, this assumes a certain kind of closeness with your boss.

+ Stop volunteering to do things you don't like to do and that won't effect your life positively. Yes, women are asked to do more support work in the workplace, but you can also stop raising your hand. This can be even tougher than saying no. The urge to be helpful and to please is powerful. But ask yourself if people in positions of power at your workplace are doing these tasks.

+ Just say no. And then offer an alternative. "I'd rather not take notes again, as I've got a lot to add to this meeting. I don't think Pete has taken notes yet—Pete, got a pencil?"

+ Practice. If you're someone who has always been agreeable, then that's what people expect of you. It takes time to re-train the people around you to expect that you're going to be looking out for yourself from now on. It's okay, they'll get over it.

+ On the home front, it's more productive to ask your part-ner to pick up a job than to complain that he or she isn't doing it. Even if your spouse really should know that you don't love booking every one of your kids' music lessons, tutors, and sports teams, if he hasn't clued in, get that done. Rather than get into a "who does more around here" battle, which will surely end badly, cut straight to the request. "I could really use your help with figuring out summer camps. Can you take that on?"

✦ It gets better. Creating boundaries for yourself can be uncomfortable (for you and those around you), but if you stick with it, you'll feel more and more at home in this new land of no.

✦ If you're a manager or on your way to becoming a manager, be sure you're not part of this problem.

Finally, as if saying no in the workplace wasn't difficult enough, oddly, with friends and family (the people who should support and understand you), it's even more difficult. I used to pride myself on being an excellent friend. I always answered the phone, I always had time to listen to any problem, I would always try my absolute best to make myself available for drinks or coffee or shopping. The problem was, the second I couldn't be available for one reason or another, I would feel an immediate resentment toward me, as if I had failed. I would then carry around this feeling all day long, plotting and planning to "make it up" to them—all the while distracting myself from the very thing I needed to get done. As I continued along this path, I noticed that more and more I felt like I was in the doghouse for disappointing people. Which really hurt, because I love these people! And yet, I started to grow resentful, because I was constantly having to compromise myself for everyone else's happiness. One day, when I was particularly upset at a raging guilt trip I had just received because I couldn't meet for a happy hour drink as a result of a looming deadline, I became furious after I hung up the phone. My mind swirled with rage as I began to categorize every thankless thing I'd ever done for any one of my family and friends. I was now mad at *everybody*. When I started to calm down, I tried to figure out how I'd gotten here. And after trying to assign blame to specific people or situations, I realized I was the common thread in every situation. I, actually, was the problem. What I had done was, out of a need to please or out of guilt, made myself available 24/7 and therefore set unrealistic expectations. People are people and we are always going to take whatever we can get—so you better set boundaries and expectations that make sense, first and foremost, for *YOU*. This, by nature, can be a little challenging, especially if you're already entrenched in unsustainable situations, but your mental health and the health of your relationships depend on your honesty and on your ability to say no with as much confidence as you say yes.

#SORRYNOTSORRY

The privilege of a lifetime is being who you are.
—JOSEPH CAMPBELL

I hear women saying *sorry* all day long in my office:

"Sorry I didn't get that report to you earlier." *It wasn't late.*

"Sorry, I took the last parking spot." *You were there first.*

"Sorry, I've got to leave the office." *It's 6 p.m., that's reasonable.*

It goes on and on. And once again, this is just one of those words that is used completely incorrectly—often as a deflection—and its use totally reduces your personal power. Now, listen, do you understand how hard this part was for me? I'm CANADIAN and a woman, for God's sake. My first word probably wasn't *mama* or *dada*—it was *sorry*. I could have been a spokesperson for the word. And as I evaluated my sorry situation, I realized the biggest problem was that I was apologizing not necessarily for what I had done, but rather for who I was. This, of course, is absolutely unacceptable. It's the type of thing that when done often enough wreaks havoc with your subconscious. The more you apologize for who you are, the further away you get from yourself. This circles right back to an earlier part of this book where you are evading the quest of not just finding out who you are and what you want, but owning it.

So I definitely feel your struggle. But if I can reevaluate my relationship with *sorry*, then anyone can.

Women's propensity for apologizing is so known, so discussed, it has its own hashtag. Start listening for it, and you'll hear it many times throughout your day, particularly if you work with or spend time with women. What are we sorry about? Everything, it would seem. We're sorry for the things we didn't do. We're sorry for the things we did. We're sorry we have to tell you something (anything—good news, bad news). The meme is so strong that shampoo brand Pantene created a commercial exploiting this habit. Even when we're not sorry, we're sorry about that: #sorrynotsorry.

Why are women so attached to the s-word? While it's true that women apologize more frequently than men, a study out of the University of Waterloo, Canada, shows that women and men apologize at about the same rate when they perceive themselves to have committed an offense. But here's the kicker: women perceive their own offenses at a much higher rate than men do. In the same study, women felt they were the victim of apology-worthy behavior as well. In general, women are more sensitive to emotional harmony (or lack of harmony) than men, and we then take on responsibility for that harmony.

The linguist Deborah Tannen points out that saying *sorry* may not be about apologizing at all. Rather, *sorry* can be used as a way to acknowledge another person's feelings, or even as a subtle prompt for the other person to make an apology as well. As women, we're acutely in tune with the emotional temperature of situations, be they professional or personal. Saying *sorry* can be a softening, the verbal equivalent of touching someone's elbow before delivering a message. Or, as the linguist Robin Lakoff describes, some women use *sorry* as a way of asking, "Is this okay?"

If it's smooth sailing we're after by loading on the apologizing, are we really apologizing at all? Or does the word do other jobs for us? There's been a fierce debate over the true meaning of *sorry* in a woman's professional vocabulary. First came a wave of articles scolding women for overseasoning their language with apologies, with business gurus encouraging women to excise the word altogether. In fact, 2016 saw the launch of a Gmail plug-in called Just Not Sorry that will hit you up with a red underline if you type *sorry* so that you may consider deleting it from your correspondence like any other error. On the flip side, cultural commentators, including Ann Friedman and Jessica Grose, among others, clapped back, saying women shouldn't have to adjust their language in an effort to reverse sexism in the workplace.

In her book *Talking from 9 to 5: Women and Men at Work*, Tannen describes the bind that women can find themselves in. If we use the language patterns considered to be female, women can be perceived as weak; if we adopt traditionally male speaking patterns, we're seen as overly aggressive.

So which of our apologies should go and which can stay? Let's start by finding our own natural baseline. Keep a *sorry* diary for one day. As best you can, make note of how many times the word comes out of your mouth. Do you use it when you might say "excuse me" (say, when you're popping your head into your boss's office)? Do you use it when someone bumps into you? Do you use it when you've made someone wait for you?

No strength is gained by not apologizing, earnestly and succinctly, for something you did wrong. If you're late for a meeting and have kept people waiting, apologize. If you committed to helping a friend but had to cancel, say sorry. But where you can afford to drop the *sorry* is as a verbal tic, when you're not really apologizing for anything other than being about to speak. And while it's true that you may be perceived differently by not depending on traditionally female speech patterns, in the end you have to ask yourself: so what? As we discussed in chapter 2, it's our own opinion we're depending on now. Our goal regarding the first **P** in the **POP System** is to strengthen our sense of self, not to apologize for it.

THE DEVIL OF ALL DEVILS:
THE WORD *SHOULD*

Guilt is to the spirit what pain is to the body.
—ELDER DAVID A. BEDNAR

And now we come to the final word that I want to draw your attention to—and then kick to the curb. *Should*. *Should* is a word that implies obligation and expectation and often comes as a box set that's gift-wrapped in guilt and even shame. It's also a word that implies an open-endedness and the absence of a decision. It describes possibility rather than reality. "I should go to the gym" is not the same as "I'm going to the gym." "I'm going to the gym" is definitive. You've got a plan and you're executing that plan. There's no feeling involved, it's simply a commitment. The person saying "I should go to the gym" might end up by lacing up her runners, or she might spend another hour on the couch. Not only does *should* suggest things are still up in the air, it's almost always a negative. We rarely use *should* when talking about something we're looking forward to. If you wanted to describe something you hoped for but weren't sure would come through, you'd say, "I hope I can make it to that conference next month" or "I want to leave the office in time to join friends for dinner." You don't have a set-in-stone plan yet in these scenarios, but your desires are clear. When you find yourself saying *should*, you're not anticipating something great, but rather are reminding yourself of that never-ending to-do list you should (there it is again!) be chipping away at.

*Should*ing ourselves is a major energy drain, as it compels us to split focus. We're forcing our minds to be in two places at once. If I'm exhausted after a marathon week and am urgently in need of a day involving my bed and a book, but I'm taunted by the feeling that I should be helping my parents clean out their garage, I'm now in two places. I'm also in neither place, really. I'm not enjoying some well-earned self-care, because I'm distracted by my guilt, and I'm not helping my parents, because I couldn't make a decision to do so. I've robbed myself of the satisfaction that either of these choices could have brought me. We're never truly in the moment if we allow thoughts of *should* to be telling us a story of another choice that might have been made.

Which brings us to *should*'s true toxic nature. We don't actually say *should* that often, not out loud, anyway. No, *should* is the word we say to ourselves, all day long. Inner dialogue is something all humans have—it's the self-talk we discussed in chapter 2. If left unchecked and untrained in the ways we worked on in the last chapter, the brain can be noisy with negative commentary. Imagine a sportscaster (except it's you!) describing your day. "Really? Can you not see the muffin top those jeans are creating? You should lose five pounds before wearing those." *Should* plays a key role in the lion's share of this trash talk. Your alarm goes off and you think, *I should go for a run . . . but I really want to sleep for fifteen more minutes.* At lunch you tell yourself, *I should order the salad . . . but I'm craving a burger.* After a phone call with you mother, you think, *I really should get out to my parents' place more often. I should go this weekend.* There's nothing wrong with wanting to exercise, eat healthy, and stay connected with our families. But the very fact of a *should* in a sentence is a red flag that you either don't want to do that thing or don't really intend to do it. Either way, you've created a divide between what you're expected to do and what you want to do. If you are saying the word *should*, but really mean something different, you are penalizing yourself—which over time will deplete you.

And whose expectations are we meeting—or worse, failing—when we badger ourselves with should? This can be a tricky tangle to unpick. But it's worth slowing down and examining if you're being pulled toward doing something because *you* believe it's the right thing to do or because you're conforming to a societal expectation that doesn't serve you.

Here are a few times you shouldn't *should*:

I **should** go to Jenny's baby shower because she went to mine. *Wrong.*

I **should** do more work on this paper because I have an extra couple of hours. *Wrong.*

I **should** go pick up the kids because my husband has had a really tough week. *Wrong.*

If you are saying the word *should* in a sentence there is a 99 percent chance you are wrong.

The only time *should* should be used is in choosing a priority or order to something that has a quantifiable outcome, e.g., "I should go to the bank before the meeting because traffic is lighter and I will waste less time."

Making changes in how we speak, and therefore in how we think, is significant. If you've been doing anything one way for years, switching gears will feel uncomfortable. And it's that discomfort that can set off alarm bells for many women. Making other people uncomfortable?

Making myself uncomfortable? It's like sirens going off in your brain! But with repetition, saying what you mean (rather than what is expected of you) can become as comfortable as your old habits were.

Here's the Drill

- ☐ Name some *yes* scenarios that you've found yourself in.

- ☐ Name at least three things you'd like to say no to.

- ☐ Write a couple of lines about how you'll say no to these things the next time they come up.

- ☐ Take note of how many times you say *sorry* on a given day. What were you apologizing for?

- ☐ Name at least three of the *should*s you've felt in the past week. What would have happened if you hadn't done these things?

CHAPTER FOUR

How the Internet Changed the Game for Women

Venice, 2009

*I*t was almost six months after I had hit rock bottom. My failed writing career (and the bullheaded approach I had employed in trying to make it work) had officially petered out and left me with nothing. (You'll read more about this in an upcoming chapter.) I had been lucky to be hired as a copywriter for a fledgling self-improvement start-up, but a couple of months in, I realized that this start-up (like most) was on shaky financial ground.

I kept my head down and worked hard. I genuinely had a very positive attitude (which frankly is a little rare for a Capricorn like me), despite weekly layoffs. I was intent on making the best of the situation and just reveled in the fact that, at least for now, I had a steady (albeit tiny) paycheck coming in each week.

My tenure at this start-up happened to coincide with the 2008 presidential election, and as the competition heated up, there would be a weekly political debate during the company lunch over campaign trail highlights. Being a "starting level" employee and the newest hire, I had had very little interaction with any of the decision makers, much less the CEO. But during these weekly lunches, thanks largely to my very spirited participation in all things political, I was noticed by the CEO. After not too long, he and I were dominating the weekly lunch meetings with our opinions and predictions. So it was with great trepidation that I entered his office, after he had requested a meeting one Thursday afternoon. I had seen with each passing week the number of layoffs increasing—no department was spared. I was sure my number was up, but I tried to focus on the positive: I had been exposed to a whole new industry and I liked what I saw.

As I sat down, the CEO informed me that the company would be closing, or sold if possible. I was shocked. I'd known things were bad, but not that bad. The second surprise, however, immediately followed. There was a tiny blog that he had just acquired from a former employee, called *Pick the Brain*. It was a little thing, but had some good early momentum. Now that he planned to sell the company, he wanted to separate *Pick the Brain* from the larger company and have it run as its own entity. And . . . *he wanted me to run it*. I didn't know what to say. I was so excited I could hardly contain myself. Why me?! I wasn't even sure what a blog was! Suffice to say, I immediately accepted and would just have to figure everything out. Six weeks later, after the office had been shut down, I sat back at my desk in my little Venice guesthouse and logged on, for the first time, to the back end of PicktheBrain.com. I was now the editor in chief—the everything in chief.

While, at first, I was totally daunted—I'd been basically computer illiterate up until a year prior—the cool thing was this was a very new space and it was just starting to explode. That meant there were many, many people trying to figure out this unfamiliar landscape, regardless of their technical abilities. Sure, I had to play catch-up and learn some basic coding and fast-track my studies in the burgeoning social media field, but if I had one thing going for me, it was that I've always been a quick study. What's more, the internet was such an exciting, fast-paced world in comparison to the molasses-slow worlds of my past writing experiences, it didn't really feel like work at all. It was totally energizing. What amazed me most—and still does to this day—was the warp speed with which the online world moves. I was forging relationships with fellow bloggers almost daily. It would have taken me months just to get a meeting (if I even could) with someone in the traditional entertainment world—but one email or "poke" on Facebook and the connection was instantaneous. What's more, there was a general camaraderie and a built-in support system online. Fellow bloggers understood quickly that forming alliances (via linkbacks and social shares), creating a weblike network, helped everyone. So if I was connected to a couple of people, I would actively support their growth, because their growth directly helped me. This mentality is the exact opposite of that of most people in traditional jobs (especially entertainment), where everyone is very protective of their gains and of the tactics used to make them. Rather than shrouding their efforts in secrecy, fellow bloggers went out of their way to share their latest growth-building hacks and techniques. As soon as something was discovered, they'd write a blog post about it and share.

Within a couple of months, I had been able to double the blog's traffic. I dove deep into the worlds of social media and also formed burgeoning networks there. It was so amazing that everything was real-time. *No waiting*. There was no taking six months to write a script, another two months to find somebody to read it, and another three months to hear back. This was: write a blog post, publish it, share it on social, and start watching the analytics. Did people like it? I'd know almost immediately. And that knowledge became invaluable. It gave me the tools I needed to be able to pivot quickly based on what was working and what wasn't. Plus, with a direct line of communication to my growing audience, I could literally give them what they were asking for. Mutual satisfaction. This was truly the democratization of hard work, being able to reach your audience directly and keep track of success in real time instead of relying upon esoteric, subjective opinions of the traditional workplace hierarchies. And for a woman, this was priceless. A boss, and his opinions of how things "should" be done, became irrelevant, because my audience had spoken.

As I continued to take *PTB* to the next level, I sat down with my old CEO and pitched an idea. I showed him the tremendous success I'd had in a very short time and told him of my boundless enthusiasm for the blog. Instead of being the editor in chief—just an employee—I told him, I *was Pick the Brain*—and wanted to be a partner. After a couple of brainstorming sessions, we worked out a deal. I had turned my stroke of good luck into a viable business. This never would have been possible offline.

Today, we have more than four hundred writers writing for us from around the world. We are read in dozens of countries daily, have been included on more than one hundred "Best of the Web" lists, have navigated a handful of Google and Facebook algorithm changes, and are still one of the most respected self-improvement blogs on the web.

POP *Truth:*

THE WEB IS WHAT YOU MAKE IT.

✦ Was the internet made for women?

✦ Are you using the internet to your greatest advantage?

✦ Can you YOLO more and FOMO less?

The internet has become such a significant part of our lives that it feels normal, like the way things are. The effects it's had on the way we live makes it feel like the air itself. Of course, it isn't. Our day-to-day reliance on the internet as a place where we can check the news, order a taxi, buy clothes, and know the dating status of our celebrity best friends is only about twenty years old. It's the blink of an eye in terms of human history. When "the information superhighway" began, it was seen as the most radical modern convenience yet. It would allow us to speed through things that used to slow us down, allow for greater freedoms, help people to connect more easily to one another, and, most vitally, democratize information and opportunity.

Like any major shift in the culture, the internet has been both praised and damned. Video killed the radio star, anyone? But for our purposes we'll take a look at what the internet and the digital age have meant to women. In my own life, it has literally meant the difference between success and failure. In the world of traditional entertainment,

I was frustrated, pushed around, stuck. I was at the mercy of forces I couldn't always understand. In the then-new age of digital publishing, I was suddenly unstoppable. Quite literally, because there was no one to stop me. If something wasn't successful at work, I'd know it immediately, change my focus, and be back on my way.

There is something about how the internet works that played to my strengths. Unlike the murky, byzantine world of traditional entertainment, the internet (or at least my corner of it) felt brightly lit and I could see a path forward. When I communicated with other content creators, they answered me back. It felt like a community rather than a battlefield. The walls that had separated professional secrets in the old landscape were knocked down. I had a boss, and then a business partner, but the people really in charge were our audience, and my ability to succeed hinged on me listening to them and what they wanted. I've always thrived in situations where ideas are volleyed back and forth—in fact, it's the very thing that struck my boss about me. I love a great discussion, and the internet delivers that instantaneous connection like nothing else.

And, was I crazy, did it seem like there were more and more women jumping into this new arena? Whether it was editorial platforms, online stores, or blogs both small and large, female-run URLs were popping up daily. Women like Sophia Amoruso (*Nasty Gal*), Heather Armstrong (*Dooce*), Garance Doré (*Atelier Doré*), and Natalie Massenet (*Net-a-Porter*) were becoming the stars of this new landscape. Their interests and points of view couldn't have been more different from each other's, but what they all shared was that they saw online an opportunity that didn't exist before.

My own business partner, Geri Hirsch, had a front-row seat for this transition. An idea she had all but abandoned after coming up against resistance in the traditional entertainment world took off in digital form. Geri had the idea for our company, LEAFtv, a long time ago and pitched it to television producers and networks. Everyone loved the idea but couldn't understand how to make it work on TV. "The frustration was that I didn't really have a way to reach the right demo. Until YouTube." Once people stopped watching shows on their TV sets and started streaming video on their devices . . . voilà! A shoppable video platform that women could access anywhere suddenly made sense.

"Really, the internet is the democratization of content—if people resonate with you, they're going to watch you. And if they don't, you're toast. It's opened up this huge lane for anybody with something to say. And I had something to say," says Geri. The other thing the internet has opened up is scale. Geri considers Sophia Amoruso: "She started taking pictures of clothes and putting them up on eBay. Would she have been able to build a multimillion-dollar business without the internet? Probably not. You can get a tiny shop on a corner in San Francisco. Is that going to be the next Victoria's Secret? Probably not. But she was able to touch on a moment in time and speak to women in a way that nobody else really was yet."

The success of Nasty Gal, one of the early online shopping sites, was like a floodgate opening for other retailers. It proved not only that women were more than willing to shop online, but that people wanted some personality along with their shopping basket. In the high-end arena, Natalie Massenet was putting the same pieces together, marrying shopping with editorial content at Net-a-Porter. And it's what we created with LEAFtv, a wellness video platform, where women could trust and connect with content and, if they wanted, also shop. This ability to connect is driving a new kind of business venture as well as developing a new kind of audience/customer, and, increasingly, women are in the driver's seat.

Women, and particularly women of color, are launching their own businesses at an increasing rate. The number of women-owned businesses in the U.S. has grown 68 percent since 2007, according to a report from the Institute for Women's Policy Research, compared to 47 percent for all businesses. With greater access to information and training that the internet provides, this number will only rise. Tech entrepreneur Jewel Burks (creator of clever app Partpic) sees the effect that the internet has had on young women. "I think it's becoming a more level playing field and the reason is because of access to information. It's so much easier to get certain information. There are still some barriers that exist. For example, you may not have internet access in your home. But as access improves, we will see the walls come down even more. For instance, you don't have to go to school for engineering to learn how to code. You can access Codeacademy. You can really teach yourself a lot of it. It makes it so people don't necessarily have to spend hundreds of thousands on a degree if they really just want to build something and make something. I think as long as you have creativity and a little hustle about you and are willing to get down and dirty and teach yourself things, you can create and you can achieve."

Launching an online business has been attractive to women in as many ways as the traditional workplace has failed them. There's an inherent flexibility to digital work. When brick-and-mortar offices were slow to allow the flextime that many women want, starting an online business that could be done anytime and anyplace had a big appeal. And even if they weren't starting businesses per se, women were racing to the internet with blogs. Blogs about parenting, beauty products, cooking, finance, politics, celebrity gossip—really, anything half the population is interested in—were spreading like wildfire. Women were using blogs as a way to communicate with the world and with each other, all the while bypassing the gatekeepers of traditional media.

Women finding a place online occurred at a critical time, marked by a steep economic downturn. We shifted from a manufacturing economy—where men had historically thrived even without college educations—to an information-driven economy, which women have proven to be well suited to. In her 2012 bestselling *The End of Men*, Hanna Rosin talks about how this shift in economy has been like gas on a fire for women. Even back in 2010 she was developing her thesis in a short but impactful TED Talk. She described the skills that were suddenly in demand in this new world order. "Intelligence, the ability to sit still and focus, communicate openly, to be able to listen to people and to be able to operate in a workplace that is more fluid than it used to be. Those are all things that women do extremely well, as we're seeing." Rosin was talking not only about the internet but about the information age, which largely takes place online. And there's no doubt in my mind that the ability to listen and communicate is what makes women so successful in the digital space.

Whether we're working, self-publishing, or just getting life done, women are online in greater numbers than men are. According to comScore, women spend 24.8 hours per month online, compared to men's 22.9. And women use the internet to connect with others more than men, spending more time on social platforms. Sixteen point three percent of women's time online is spent on social media compared to 11.7 percent of men's time. You could say that women are more in touch with the essence of the online experience. Women make up a larger part of the population on social media. More women than men use Facebook, Instagram, and Pinterest (but more men use YouTube and

LinkedIn). These are all platforms that respond to communication and exchange, and women, raised as communicative empaths, flourish there.

In these overscheduled times, and with women often stuck with the lion's share of domestic and family chores, we can use the internet to ease our burdens. Getting through your own to-do list is hard enough, but add to that the running of a household and emotionally supporting everyone in it, and productivity can feel like a bridge too far. But the internet has the potential to take some of those tasks off our plates, so that we're spending our time at home (and with loved ones) as productively as we can. It really defeats the purpose to be razor focused on how you're spending your time and energy all day at work, only to throw out that concept as soon as you walk through your front door. We can order groceries to be delivered to our doors, book a kid's birthday party, find a plumber, and book next year's ski trip. But, women being women, we also have the tendency to use the internet as a way to just pile on more obligations as well as to check how our lives are stacking up against those of others.

The internet is good for women. Mostly. We've harnessed its power. Kinda. We're using it to advance our own goals. Sometimes.

So are we winning on the internet? Let's do this the old-fashioned way, shall we?

PROS

Flexibility. The digital age means that work, depending on the kind of job a person does, can be done anywhere. Flextime and the ability to work from home have been advantages for women (if they work for companies agreeable to them). But it's not just work that can be done anywhere. The rest of our lives can also come with us to work. And being able to use a break from work to order groceries or send out e-vites to an upcoming birthday party is another bit of flexibility women use to make their lives run more efficiently.

Outsourcing. Have a task you want off your to-do list? It's very likely there's someone out there willing to do it. For a price, of course. Few of us would dream of having a full-time personal assistant, but on sites like Upwork and Freelancer you can find thousands of contractors looking to pick up work handling expenses, booking appointments, planning travel, etc. And of course, you can go online to find a reputable dog walker, handyman, housecleaner, and more.

Control. Getting things started—whether it's an editorial website, a consulting business, or a portfolio to show off your work—is just easier online. If it's something that's new to you, someone out there has created a video tutorial for it. You don't have to ask anyone's permission to get things done online.

Connection. Having a life that is moving full-tilt can make it hard to stay in touch with those we aren't really invested in. But there is something great about being able to see what your cousin in Berlin is doing for her birthday this year, even if you can't make it to her party.

CONS

The comparison trap. We're not just online connecting and buying—we're often online comparing. The study of upward and downward social comparison existed long before the internet. Humans seem to be born with the desire to assess themselves by comparing themselves with others. When we compare ourselves to those we perceive as more accomplished or better off, we're engaging in upward social comparison. When we compare ourselves to those we consider less successful, we're engaging in downward social comparison. The internet, and social media in particular, has put this tendency on steroids. Flicking through Instagram and seeing sun-soaked holiday snaps ("She looks so much better in a bikini than I do!") can become a way of torturing ourselves rather than merely staying in touch with friends.

The longest leash. Yes, email and the internet mean you can work from home, but they also mean your employer may feel it's appropriate to expect you to be available for work at any hour of the day. It's not at all unusual for many of us to be on an email thread for work that is still bouncing around at 9:30 p.m. And as long as some show-off is responding, then everyone feels like they have to. In early 2017 France passed a law stating that work emails outside of work hours are no longer acceptable labor practice, allowing employees to have truly off-work time. No such law exists in North America.

FOMO. Before we lived our lives online—or at least showed them off online—you might have felt a twitch of regret over staying in on a Saturday night when you knew your friends were hitting the town. The internet has introduced two new elements to this experience. One is that people make selective use of their social media, sharing mostly filtered, #blessed moments. Lots of lattes, smiling children, cute outfits of the day, and cozy tableaus featuring blankets, teacups, and artfully torn jeans. Oh, and then there are the vacations. Two is that we're not just following our actual friends on social media. Platforms like Instagram make it easy to keep an envious eye on every stripe-shirted style blogger from Amsterdam, every yummy mummy from Australia and yoga model in Aruba. Put those together and it's possible to dine on a jealousy sandwich any day of the week.

Obligation. If you have a large network online, you probably also feel a large amount of pressure to like every image of someone's new puppy, lol at every goofy joke, and forward every meme. Just writing this made me want a nap.

Sexism. For every kick-ass feminist who has used the internet as a way to articulate women's experience in a new and intelligent way, there's a death-/rape-threatening troll living rent-free in his mother's basement trying to terrorize her. Many of the internet's lady heroes— Kelly Oxford, Jamilah Lemieux, Lauren Duca—clap back and keep doing their important work. But others grow weary of the relentless threats and stupidity—Lindy West, Anita Sarkeesian, and temporarily, Jessica Valenti—and step away from social media. The abovementioned women were involved in dramatic scenarios, but most women who have logged onto Twitter can share a story or two of misogynistic insults being flung at them. The internet has given a platform to women, and one day one of them will MacGyver a way to neutralize these losers, but not yet.

YOU AND THE INTERNET

How can you make sure that you're using your time online in a way that supports your goals rather than distracts or diminishes you? Apps like RescueTime allow you to get an honest accounting of how you're using your online time. Most of us probably think that the bulk of our time online is work-related, but up to 40 percent of our time online is spent on social media. This kind of time-tracking app can show you the reality of how your days are really spent. And once you get those results, be honest with yourself about how time spent on various digital platforms makes you feel. Do you feel bad about yourself when you see on Instagram that two friends went on a hike without you this morning? Does your heart sink when you see the holiday snaps your ex-boyfriend posted on Facebook? Does having a quick exchange on Twitter with a friend mean that you won't bother following up about that dinner you keep promising to book?

An analysis of forty studies, conducted by the Graduate Institute of Education in Changhua, Taiwan, showed the internet has a small but significant negative impact on general well-being. A German study showed that Facebook can be a stressful environment that encourages feelings of envy and decreases users' sense of life satisfaction. Another study out of the University of Pittsburgh's Center for Research on Media, Technology, and Health found a strong relationship between excessive time on social media and depression. And particularly for those prone to depression, social media can be an even darker place. If you're feeling down and looking to social media for support, you may end up feeling worse when you encounter people's happy vacation snaps. Other researchers counter that social media can increase people's trust and engagement with each other and with political events. The difference in these findings seems to lie in an important factor: action. People who lurk on social media, simply taking in images and posts, tend to be brought down by the experience. Those who engage—write comments on posts, or post images or articles themselves—feel connected and happier for the experience.

One thing can't be said: that our time online is neutral. It's a key step in your process to consider how your time online affects you. Are you drained by it? Are you informed by it?

How to Lessen Your Online Distractions

1 *Disable the culprits!* If you know—from doing your homework—that you're answering the siren call of Pinterest or your favorite online retailer, then address the problem. You can either block them completely or set up a block on a timer, like SelfControl, so that you can only go on at scheduled times.

2 *Gather together all the tasks you can do offline* and then shut off your Wi-Fi for part of the day.

3 *Set a schedule, which includes distractions.* Knowing that you can go and poke around social media during your scheduled break at two thirty will help you keep on task until then.

4 *Make your current work full screen.* Don't allow the visual presence of tabs for Facebook, Twitter, and Apartment Therapy lure you away at every micro pause.

5 *Stop following and/or engaging with people who bring you down.* You can be affected by people even through the interface of social media. If you find yourself rolling your eyes each time you see a colleague's avatar on Twitter, go ahead and un-follow.

For me, the internet provided a clear path to success that previously wasn't available to me. Not only were there tools there to help me get started, but it turns out that this type of environment works way better with my temperament and the lifestyle I wanted to have. Furthermore, when I first began with my other business, LEAFtv, my partner and I needed a proof of concept before we could get taken seriously in any way. So how would we do that? Easy. There were no barriers to entry, no applications to fill out—we didn't need to be accepted by anyone or anything. We simply began producing video content on a shoestring budget, editing, uploading, and watching in real time to see if people responded to what we were doing. This kind of efficiency and ease of entry into a brand-new market was never even close to available to me (or anyone) before the internet. It has revolutionized the way we do business and how we get things done. I also believe that the unfettered access—which allowed me to try and fail without anyone's permission—specifically benefited me as a woman. Either our content was good or it wasn't. And we got paid for each view, the same as any man—which, as we know by now, does not reflect traditional workplace salary structures.

Here's the Drill

☐ Track your online time with an app like RescueTime and analyze the results.

☐ Name three ways that you're able to use the internet to make your life run more efficiently.

☐ Name three times social media has made you feel worse rather than better.

☐ List three ways you could organize your online time to support you rather than control you.

PART TWO

Doing

How to POP Your Productivity

CHAPTER FIVE

Why You Should Stop Doing Everything and Start Focusing on Just Three Areas (Seriously)

Los Angeles, fall 2001: *City of Broken Glass*

One week after 9/11, my best friend and I drove across the border, headed due south from the Canadian prairies to Los Angeles, the City of Broken Dreams, confident we would be the exceptions, not the rule. Canada is perhaps one of the most patriotic places on earth, but as I drove through a sea of American flags, proudly represented on every car we passed—a show of solidarity after the horrors that had just happened—I felt awestruck in the face of such unity and power. I felt like an outsider, but now more than ever, I wanted in.

We had a dream and boundless enthusiasm—*but that was about it*. When we arrived a week later, we found the dark, run-down West L.A. apartment where we would begin our adventures in couch surfing for the next two months, and began to settle in. After yet another week or two of playing tourist in our new town, being shown around by the only two other people we knew here, we were experiencing peak excitement. We could feel the sense of possibility. The energy screamed, *Anything could happen!* Each night after another exhausting, exhilarating day of rollerblading around the Venice boardwalk, lunching in Beverly Hills, having drinks in Hollywood, we would return to our dark little nook and talk about all the *could-be*s in our near future. And each night, right before my eyes closed, I wondered to myself when everything would start happening for us.

I awoke one morning with the solid realization that if anything was indeed going to happen, it wouldn't come from waiting. We would have to start making a plan of sorts.

So with great gusto, we decided that morning that we would start taking care of business. We would open our bank accounts and start down the path to responsibility. We gathered up all the ID we would need—passports and driver's licenses, all our cash—and headed out. We had also decided that morning that we would get in a hike up Runyon Canyon—a famed L.A. hiking spot over in Hollywood. As we packed up the car, we decided it would make more sense to go hiking first, before it got too hot, and then head over to the bank.

As we wound up the final, steep leg of the canyon, I was excited, feeling we were going to be one step closer to our dream of *making it* in Hollywood. I parked the car in a dust-filled, makeshift lot at the top of the mountain and hopped out. To be safe, we put all our valuables in the trunk, locked the car, and skipped off for some mildly smog-soaked fresh air. As we powered our way down and then back up the red-clay terrain, we marveled at the incredible view and the power of the city below us. We mused on all the amazing things we had in store for us. Breathless, back up at the top of the hill, we dusted ourselves off, took one last look out over our future, and then headed back to the car. I believe we were midway through discussing what Jamba Juice we would have for lunch when, in the distance, I saw my car but noticed something strange: the front window was an iridescent turquoise blue. I squinted, trying to make out the reason why. Was the sun playing tricks? I nudged my friend to see if she saw the same thing. "Hmmm. Weird," she said after cloning my squint.

The dust began to kick up as my leisurely, post-workout stroll turned into a fast-paced gallop. As we arrived at the car, my jaw dropped. My head spun. The window in question was now only half there, made up of jagged broken glass. The remainder covered the ground around the front of the car.

"What the hell?!" my friend exclaimed as she arrived at my side. "Why would anyone do this?!"

And as the last question mark hung off her lips, my heart stopped and my mouth went dry.

"The trunk," I said, in a barely audible whisper. She looked up at me, saucers for eyes.

The five-step walk from the driver's-side door to the back of the car was one of the longest I have ever taken. As we stood squarely before the trunk, my hands shook as I popped it, then, as if in slow motion, lifted it up. As one, we gasped.

It was empty. Everything was gone. Our driver's licenses, our passports, our phones, and yes, all our cash, was gone.

I could hear my scream echo all the way down the canyon.

At over sixty miles an hour, I flew down the side of the mountain, winding back and forth, dodging oncoming traffic as shards of broken glass ricocheted like bullets inside the car. We didn't speak a word. We had to get off this fucking mountain and to a phone. *We didn't even have a quarter for a pay phone.* Our very few options rattled in my head with each swerve and bump. Forty-five minutes later we were outside a friend's apartment in Century City, climbing in through a side window he'd left open for the day. As I collapsed on his kitchen floor, exhausted and out of breath, I could see a telephone on the counter. I scrambled over, filthy and bleeding, to start making calls. I quickly discovered that in the two hours since we had started our Runyon Canyon roller coaster, over $10,000 had been spent on the "emergency" AmEx my parents had lent me. And that was the best news that I would receive in the coming days.

Just under two weeks later, we realized we had been caught up in a nightmare, a spiderweb of problems. We couldn't get new credit cards because we had no IDs. We didn't have our driver's licenses, so driving was a risk (made worse by the fact that we had Winnipeg plates). We couldn't accept an emergency thousand-dollar wire my parents tried to send us, as we had no IDs and couldn't get the money out. Even in our exceptional circumstance, there were no exceptions to these rules. The final blow came late on a Friday afternoon as the one entity I still hoped could get us out of this mess, the Canadian consulate, let us know that not only could they not issue us temporary passports so that we could have *one* piece of ID, but their rules had changed. Since 9/11 (just over a month earlier), anyone whose passport had been stolen had to immediately return home—our country of birth would be the only place that could issue new documentation, and we couldn't stay in the United States without the proper paperwork.

In short, the Canadian consulate demanded we go back to Canada.

By Sunday, after a thousand rivers of tears had been cried, my partner in crime decided she couldn't do this any longer and would go back. She promised she would return as soon as she sorted everything out— but we both knew that wasn't true.

Unfortunately/fortunately for me, less than six weeks in, there was just no scenario in which going back to Canada made sense for me. I knew that if I went back, the same fate that awaited my friend would be mine: I would never come back. And that just wasn't an option. I knew I had come for a reason—I just no longer knew (if I ever did) what that was.

So I dug in my heels and decided, now totally alone, that I would stay.

This time, however, I would need a fucking plan.

POP *Truth:*

LESS IS A LOT MORE.

+ Choose your goals.

+ Not too many.

+ Don't do anything else (when you can avoid it).

Now, what happened to me that ominous day at the top of Runyon Canyon could easily be dismissed as bad luck. And though it definitely was terrible luck, I would say this example, though extreme, highlights a much larger problem. And a solution. When you act without a thought-out plan, you are completely at the mercy of the world around you. If it's kind to you, you might scrape by for a while. But if it's not, you can lose everything. And when you are trying to make a plan, if your goals are vague—e.g., "to make it in Hollywood"—it becomes impossible to move forward. You are chasing something that is in the clouds—a pretty view from the top of a dusty canyon—that you will never be able to pull down to earth. These aren't goals at all, because they're not reality-based. They're dreams. And trying to give them oxygen just kills them. Dead.

Perhaps what is equally important, and maybe a little counterintuitive, is that the creating of a plan is not actually the difficult part. What is very challenging is deciding which dreams you're going to follow. Once you've landed on specific goals you can create a path, complete with expectations for yourself. But first, you will be forced to ask yourself a lot of questions that might make you uncomfortable. You may find yourself having to give up on something that you always thought you wanted. This is hard. Trust me, I know from firsthand experience. But I promise, if you do the work right, right from the beginning, you won't find yourself crying in the foothills of, as my dad renamed it, the City of Broken Glass, but rather creating a bright, shiny diamond to guide you for the rest of your life.

WHAT DO YOU WANT?

True success, true happiness lies in freedom and fulfillment.
—DADA VASWANI

If your life was an apartment, you'd be looking around thinking it's looking pretty sweet about now. You've done a major purge: packed up the psychology textbooks from college you're never going to look at again, tossed the boyfriend jeans that never fit in the first place, and thrown away that dusty stack of DVDs (I mean, come on). Metaphorically, of course! Your metaphoric apartment may not be perfect yet, but clearing out the junk has made a world of difference. Marie Kondo became an international sensation a couple of years back by introducing us to her philosophy of the life-changing qualities of tidying up. Kondo had people filling up dumpsters in response to a single, simple question when it came to belongings: does it bring you joy?

That's exactly what you did in part one of this book. You got honest about what kind of person you are and what you require to feel happy and fulfilled. Then you cross-checked that against your life and took a hard look at what's truly serving you and what isn't. Getting rid of guilt, obligation, the opinions of others, and the need to please is literally making space for you.

Now that we've cleared the mental, emotional, and *actual* space amid all that clutter that was slowing us down, it's time to build. But this time, we're going to do things differently. Rather than fill up your time with everyone else's agendas, we're going to create one that's all you. Of course, I can't say you can just quit your job and stop doing laundry, but you can radically reorder your time and energy. And we're going to do it by being strategic. We're going to do less. That still sounds strange, right? The whole world is urging us on to more, more, more! Get in that workout! Go the extra mile at work! Bake those cookies! But remember what we talked about in chapter 3? We're saying no, no, no to more, more, more. The myth of multitasking is what had us stretched thin to the point of collapse.

Becoming awesome at something takes a lot of work. A recent study out of Princeton University may have debunked Malcolm Gladwell's ten-thousand-hours theory of mastery (showing that this notion was very much dependent on the area of life you're focused on) but there's no doubt that the more time and focus you can put into something, the more you'll get out of it. It's one of the cruelest traps that our culture has laid out for women in forcing them to do so much more than men; we become the Jills-of-all-trades, masters of none. In ditching the idea that we have to do everything, we open the door to crushing a few things that we truly care about.

THREE THINGS

The rule of three is so universally appealing to people that it applies to art, education, and presentations, to name a few (well, three, actually). We like to see objects arranged in threes, and we like to hear information presented in a sequence of three ideas. Three is the smallest number that can indicate a pattern. There is something both manageable and elegant about the number three that strikes a chord with humans. You'll find many versions of this approach but the basic concept is always the same: be clear about the few things that are most important to you. Applying a laser focus to a small list of goals means you'll be moving forward on those goals, not inching along on them and a hobo sack of other things you don't really care about.

WHY THREE THINGS?

We know that if the mainstream culture had its way with us, women would be so dizzy with all the costume changes we're asked to make in a day—mother, CEO, PTA leader, yogini, community builder, wife, friend, lover—we could barely walk a straight line. Oh, wait, that's already the case! Deciding consciously to focus on three key goals allows you the mental space to mute the dull roar of other, less productive tasks. Seriously, imagine how much you could accomplish regarding the goals you truly care about if you didn't have fifteen other plates to keep spinning.

Three is a particularly good number of things to focus on at a time because it's reasonable. It's sane. You can do three things in concert without feeling overwhelmed or confused. Of course it could be two things and yes, of course it could be four. But when you get into bigger groups of goals you're going to feel that familiar stress and exhaustion creep back in.

UM, WHAT THINGS?

No lie, this is tricky. Just remember, you're only choosing three things for now. These aren't objectives you have to commit to for life. You can isolate three things to focus on for a year, or even six months. But choose goals with enough meat on the bone for at least six months. We're not talking about a list that has "eat more vegetables" (although totally eat more vegetables!) or "tidy up the medicine cabinet." Think about what makes your heart race. What would make your life better? What do you want? Go ahead and go big with these. Don't worry about how you'll get there—we'll handle that later in the book.

Here are some examples:

Research and draft a business plan for my dream project.

Get pregnant.

Go back to school for interior design.

Renovate apartment.

Commit to exercise five times a week.

Establish a new routine at home with my family (so I'm not doing everything).

Buy a house.

Become a manager in my company.

Rebuild a relationship with my mother (we've been in an unspoken standoff for years).

Move to L.A.

Quit my job as publicist and find a new one in the nonprofit sector.

Travel to South America and see the places where my parents grew up.

Write the novel I've been thinking about for five years.

Go ahead and make a list that has more than three goals, if more than three come to you. We're going to cross some out in a minute. Remember, not all three things that you choose as your goals need to have the same weight or value. Starting your own business and getting into great shape may seem lopsided, but if they both matter to you, include both. What does matter is that you're specific. The more clearly you can articulate what it is you're dreaming of, the easier it will be to build a plan to get you there. Those details will also tell you what you're drawn to in your goals. If I see "become a manager at my company," I know that you want to develop leadership skills and grow within the structure of your existing job. If you'd written down "get a promotion," I wouldn't know much more than that.

Finally, once you've made your preliminary list, it's important to understand that when starting to make the short list, each of your three things should generally fall within one of three large, sweeping categories: career growth, personal growth, and relationship growth. While there are some smaller headlines on the periphery, my feeling is that these are the three main channels to growth, fulfillment, balance, and a productive life. After looking at your short list, break it down as best you can, into these three filters. Ideally, you will have something in each bucket. But if you're at a particular stage in your life where career is everything, maybe you have two in that bucket and one in personal growth. To have all three in the career category, however, is something that needs to be evaluated. While it may help you to get to where you want to go to in the short term by getting a lot done, in the long term this lack of balance will leave you out on a limb, very vulnerable and exhausted. The idea here is to ultimately find balance between these three buckets, over time.

By the time you're done, your list should look something like this:

Career Growth
Launch an e-commerce site for my essential oils business.

Personal Growth
Make time for shut-off digital detox at least twice a week.

Relationship Growth
Decide whether my partner is the right one for me long term,
by conscientiously spending meaningful time together, weekly
(at least one day date, one night date).

CHECK YOURSELF

Before you set those goals in stone, you need to check them against some of the work you've already done. Remember back in chapter 1 when you did a personal inventory? Take another look at the sentence you wrote down. Does the kind of person you are and the goals you have fit together?

For instance, if you created a statement about yourself that said "I'm someone who thrives within structure, knowing what's coming up and how I can best contribute to a team" and your goal is to travel alone and write a book, then you've got some thinking to do. Is your sense of your self evolving? Maybe you're more adventurous than you gave yourself credit for. Or is a solo trip and an author credit something you wrote in your diary at fourteen and that notion never quite left you, even as your character developed in another direction? Either answer is cool, but you have to know the answer in order to move forward.

Oh, and before anyone uses this exercise as an opportunity to indulge in guilt and her ugly pal shame, forget it. Altering either your goals or your sense of yourself is not an excuse to beat yourself up. Moving toward what feels right to you and what matches your values is what this whole process is about. That you've realized you love being part of a team rather than being the brooding artist of your adolescent fantasies? It's all good news. You're one step closer to wasting less of your own time.

But maybe your personal statement was more along the lines of "I love a challenge and I don't get discouraged easily. I'm most engaged when I'm surrounded by change." Going back to school, moving to another city, or starting up your own business feels like a fit, and you'll be working with your personality rather than against it.

REGRETS, YOU'LL HAVE A FEW

Most people don't plan to fail; they fail to plan.
—JOHN L. BECKLEY

In this phase of the book, and the process of moving forward in your life, we're building an action plan. Rubber is hitting the road. It's very exciting. But because we're human—and particularly because we're human women—it's important to acknowledge that making choices can come with some sadness, too. There was probably a time in your life—teens and early twenties, maybe—where time felt infinite. Why worry about making tough choices when you'll never get a bit older? Weren't we all going to be young forever? I know I was.

Except, you know . . . it's not true. Time does move forward and we can't be all the things we ever thought we might be. We can be so many things in the course of a lifetime but we can't be everything. You can't be a world-traveling vagabond and a hard-driving CEO and a mother and a gardener. You have to choose. Something has to give. For ambitious people in particular, this truth can bristle. Weren't we raised on the rallying cry of having it all? Why the hell can't we do everything?! Um, because of the space-time continuum. Sorry about that.

In fact, now would probably be as good a time as any to address my thoughts on this notion of *having it all*—for all the leaner-inners out there. If I've learned anything, it's that we need to immediately let go of this notion, the pursuit of which is totally unrealistic and completely counter to achieving happiness or real productivity. Trying to have it all means constantly chasing something. It's an endless to-do list, with nothing on the other side except more to do. Think about it philosophically—what would happen if you did "have it all"? No more challenge, no more adventure, no more character building. It is out of the struggle and in the face of challenge that our true selves are revealed—where the most interesting parts or qualities come alive. It is in the birth and the discovery of these parts that our energy lies.

Moreover, "having it all" is vague. It's another pie-in-the-sky idea that has no real grounding in reality. It's another *concept*, full of mostly letdown, without an actionable plan. That's the problem with going for everything—oftentimes you're left exhausted and feeling empty. It's time to let things go. What's that song again, about if you take some time . . . you might just get what you need?

So what do you do with the items that have to fall off your list? Well, first, there's no shame in mourning them. It does suck that we can't have lives running concurrently. But it's clear what happens to us when we try to jam too much into the one life we do get. You can use the sadness you might feel in prioritizing your goals to help shape your list. What can you *not* strike off? If the thought of not doing something is too heartbreaking to face, then you know it's something that stays on your three-goal list. And because a dream or goal doesn't make the final cut doesn't mean you have to forget about it. Maybe it moves onto a list you come back to in ten or twenty years? Life *is* actually long, if we do it right or are lucky.

HOW TO CULTIVATE RESTRAINT

The ideas are louder when there are fewer of them.
—DAVID C. DAY

In order to get on board with the Big 3 and have it really work for you, you have to not do more than your Big 3. And it's going to be hard, particularly for the type A's, the pleasers, the good girls, the hard workers . . . you know, all of us. In order to focus on your goals, you're going to have to consistently not do other things.

I want you to picture something for a minute. Imagine all the requests that come in daily for singer, actress, designer, and philanthropist Rihanna. She must get asked to perform, endorse, donate, appear, and speak all day long. She must field an absolute avalanche of requests. And you know that someone on her team has the job of vetting these requests. Just imagine some sleekly dressed, smart-mouthed assistant flipping through gold-plated invitations, like, *nope, ha ha, as if, that's nice but not happening, now this looks good!* She's tossing most of those inquiries straight into a gilded trash bin. She knows Rihanna's priorities and doesn't even bring to her boss requests that don't meet the criteria. That would be a big waste of everyone's time. Now, we can't all have full-time assistants acting as our gatekeepers, but you can certainly start acting as your own. You can even imagine, when demands on your time come in, that you're judging the request on behalf of a VIP. Because you are. Once you've decided on your top three, this ability to step outside yourself and become ruthlessly objective about everything coming your way (much as a full-time assistant would) is crucial and actually very cathartic once you get started.

In chapter 3 we talked about how difficult it can be to say no to things, even if they're things we don't want. Restraint is a similar-but-not-exactly-the-same practice. Yes, you're going to continue saying no (when you can) to the requests that don't serve you. But restraint means that you also won't follow every idea or impulse either. You're going to consistently hold up ideas and impulses to the Big 3 test. If your three goals are "write a novel, commit to exercise, and spend quality time with my kids," then that list is what you're comparing every demand for your time against. Does working the bake sale bring you closer to your daughter? Nope. But baking cookies with her and dropping them off for the bake sale gets that job done.

You may be as addicted as the rest of the free world to binge-worthy television. And few things feel better after a long day than sinking into the couch and letting a compelling narrative wash over you. But if you want the narrative of your novel to manifest, you're going to put those hours toward writing, not watching.

Self-discipline often gets a bad rap. Who wants to be the wet blanket who heads home after one glass of wine with the girls because you've got an early Pilates class the next day? Or the killjoy who orders kale salad when everyone else is digging into pizza? We imagine that staying on the straight and narrow may deliver us the results we want, but by way of bummer abstention. Not so, discovered Wilhelm Hofmann and his team of researchers at the University of Chicago. Looking at the ability to refrain from acting on impulse and instead making choices that line up with previously made decisions made people happier not only *about* their lives but *in* their lives. You can imagine someone who can maintain their diet to feel proud of themselves for sticking to it, but you might not expect them to be happy *while* sticking to it. Hoffman discovered that people with a developed sense of self-control experienced happiness in regard to both effort and results.

When you're trying to develop a sense of restraint or self-discipline, don't expect it to come naturally. If, up until now, you've responded to what's in front of you rather than made a plan and acted on it, that's what you're good at. You can get good at working toward your Big 3 goals, too.

A FEW WAYS TO MAKE IT EASIER

1 *Habits are easier than decisions.* This is big. A habit is a behavior you perform without having to think about it. You don't decide each day whether to brush your teeth—you just brush your teeth. If you ask yourself if, after work, you should go for a run or flick through Instagram for an hour, then you might choose the

option that doesn't support your goals. Of course, it takes time to create habits, and you'll have to make decisions to get there. But the sooner you can get to always—as in, "I always work out before going into the office"—the less emotional mental friction you'll create for yourself.

2 *Remove temptation.* There are no points being handed out for unnecessary suffering. If you're trying to get lean for summer, you don't pack your freezer with ice cream. Think about your goals and what kinds of temptations you can get out of your way. Again, much of this comes down to upfront planning and knowing where you're going. If you're saving for a down payment on a house, the temptation you need to avoid is financial. So take a few minutes to unsubscribe to the dozens of emails we all get from J.Crew, Everlane, and Intermix. Even if you weren't going to buy those jeans, why remind yourself of what you're not allowed right now? Maybe the temptation you need to avoid is interpersonal and you know you have a hard time turning down requests from your boss to do work outside your job description. If you know you're going to crumble once you step in her office to explain why you don't want to organize the staff party, then send her an email where you can lay out your thoughts without emotion. Always think about putting yourself in the best possible, least stressful position to succeed.

3 *Look after yourself.* Hunger and fatigue weaken our resolve, not just when it comes to diet, but in regard to all our choices. Making new choices in your life is hard, and you need to be in fighting form to make that commitment. If you're exhausted, it's going to be much harder to stick to your guns when a tough choice comes up. This may seem simple, but I can't tell you the number of times I've caved on things, just because I was distracted by a gnawing hunger or depleted energy. Feeling tempted to buy those jeans? Drink a tall glass of room-temperature water and then see how you feel. Seriously, dehydration will make a person do crazy things. Checking in with yourself physically is important, and often a barometer for how we are feeling emotionally. Being able to address these physical concerns in real time with relatively short fixes (eating nourishing foods consistently, taking short walks throughout the day, drinking enough water) can make all the difference as you start to turn your decisions into habits.

It is in the creating of this productivity blueprint that you will not only formulate a concrete set of goals but further understand who you are and what you really want. *Only then can true productivity begin.*

#TBT TO THE CITY OF BROKEN GLASS

Would I have still ended up in Los Angeles if I had taken the time to carve out my path in advance? Maybe.

Would I have still ended up in tears at the top of a dusty mountain—all my valuables stolen? It's possible—but not probable.

What would have certainly been different was the fallout afterward. Having a concrete plan—to which you are accountable—doesn't mean nothing bad can or will ever happen to you. What it does promise, however, is the perspective and clarity you need to get through the tough stuff and stay on course without getting bogged down in the crazy anxiety of not knowing which way is up, or totally smothered by overwhelming, vague goals that are not firmly rooted in reality. Furthermore, having a well-thought-out, balanced plan does tend to open you up to more of the good stuff and to humming along, by minimizing your chances of being in the wrong place at the wrong time.

Here's the Drill

☐ Make a list of all your goals. Be sure to include goals from different aspects of your life, from personal to professional to relationships. Large and small—write them all down.

☐ Start crossing things out. Leave only what fires you up the most. Choose a single goal in each category: career growth, personal growth, relationship growth.

☐ Do these goals line up with the personality statement you created in chapter 1?

CHAPTER SIX

The Importance of Outsourcing

Venice, 2015: *Losing my religion*

As I weaved through a very congested Whole Foods aisle, small beads of sweat were building on my upper lip. I was in the thick of the Friday afternoon shopping-for-the-weekend crowd and quietly cursed myself for even *thinking* an impromptu dinner with my partner Louis's new work colleague and his wife, at the end of yet another very long week, was a good idea.

We had been kindly invited to their house for dinner a couple of weeks earlier, where we were served a lovely, very thoughtful meal by our hostess, a stay-at-home mom. She had done everything perfectly, from the appetizers to the décor to the cocktails to the meal. Over dinner, she told me how nervous she had been to cook for me, as she was a huge fan of LEAF and was terrified that she wouldn't meet my standards. I laughed out loud and told her she had far surpassed my expectations . . . and my skill level.

So two weeks later, as I was planning the night's menu, I fretted that I would have to do something spectacular to live up to my reputation. *What would be the most impressive?* Naturally, I decided to make one of the most complex dishes I could find—a traditional French dish, beef bourguignon. And to really add a layer of unnecessary anxiety, I invited Louis's good friend, a semiprofessional French chef, and his wife to join in the fun. In doing so, I also invited the criticism that would accompany a Canadian YouTuber daring to try to re-create this French masterpiece. On the way to Whole Foods I called Louis to tell him of my master plan, and how much work it was going to take, to which he responded:

"*Bébé*, you sound so stressed, why don't we just order a salad pizza and drink some rosé?"

Like it was just that simple!

"Are you nuts?! I am doing this for YOU!" I yelled as I hung up. With the guests arriving in only a handful of hours, this level of stupidity I didn't have the time for.

So now I was soldiering on alone, trying to get through this monster shopping list and endless line at the cash register, and then attempting to escape the ongoing social experiment of the Whole Foods parking lot on a Friday afternoon. By the time I got home, and before I even started my mad experiment, I was exhausted and totally frustrated.

In the kitchen, I was no more relaxed. I hurled orders at Louis and then yelled when he didn't do things exactly as I would have. Finally, I found it easier to just go it alone, which Louis had *absolutely* no problem with.

About halfway through the recipe, I started to find my rhythm, and as the Burgundy began to burn off in the pot and out into the air, I relaxed . . . *a little*. I had this under control. The glass of Burgundy I had poured for myself was also helping. I worked on the salad dressing, warmed the bread in the oven, and set the table.

To add to the ridiculousness of this story, *I don't eat meat*, so I needed somebody else to taste it. I couldn't ask Louis, because he is universal in his praise for everything I cook, even when it's terrible. I needed the voice of somebody who could be very, very critical: a French chef. I asked JB (our French friend) to come over a little early.

JB and his wife (and my good friend), Megan, arrived a couple of minutes later. Immediately upon entering the house, he wrinkled his nose, took a deep inhale of the smell in the room, and made a funny face.

"How long haz eet been cooking for?" he asked.

I went into a complete body sweat.

"I . . . uh . . . like, fifty minutes, I think?" I stammered.

"Hmmmm," he said in a tone that felt *way* too judgmental to be coming this soon, even from somebody French.

I immediately regretted my decision to not have Louis tell me how delicious the food tasted and what a great cook I was. All the confidence I had built up over the past hour or so of cooking and smelling and Burgundy-ing was gone.

As JB followed me into the kitchen, I wondered if it was too late to cancel. Of course it was—*one of the guests was already in my kitchen*. With great hesitation, I pulled the top off the large cast-iron pot and offered to ladle up a little bite for *zee food critic*. He gently nudged me out of the way, grabbing the spoon out of my hand. He began to stir the stew, diligently checking its consistency. Consistency? I hadn't focused one iota on that! I was merely navigating my way through this recipe based on a simple smell test. I shriveled down into the makeshift outfit I had thrown together. Gently, he scooped a tiny spoonful up from the steaming pot. He smelled it, then blew on it to cool it slightly. With every millisecond that passed I wanted to scream, *Can we pick up the pace here? I've still gotta do my makeup!* Finally, he placed the spoon in his mouth, closed his eyes . . . *and then tasted, I guess?* There was a long, dramatic pause, until finally his eyes popped open, a surprised look on his face. He furled his brow and then quickly fished another spoonful, this time much bigger, out of the pot. He gobbled it down. I could barely breathe.

"Eetz good," he said, in almost total disbelief.

"What?!" I gasped.

"No, reeeealy. Eetz quite good. *Très bien.*"

With that, he walked over to the table, grabbed a piece of bread, and brought it back to dip it in the sauce, nodding his head as he munched.

I couldn't believe it! *All my fuss for nothing,* I thought to myself as I hurriedly swiped on my makeup in the bathroom. *I really was amazing. I was happy to be throwing this impromptu dinner party, after all.*

The doorbell rang and I chasséed over to greet our new friends. I served them delicious wine and cocktails. They nibbled on simple yet sophisticated appetizers. Great music was playing in the background. Great conversation was being had. Everyone commented on how wonderful dinner smelled, and I beamed.

"Oh, it's nothing," I said with total false humility. "I hope it tastes okay." I winked at JB.

Finally, I had the guests all seated. Wineglasses filled. I brought over the pièce de résistance and generously served everyone a heaping bowlful. Mouths watered.

"Wait, what are you eating, Erin?" the colleague's wife asked me.

"Oh, I don't eat meat, so I'm just going to have some salad and some more bread and cheese. It's fine!"

"Really?" She looked at me like I was completely nuts.

"I do this all the time!" I said, trying to downplay what was actually kind of nuts.

I quickly raised my glass to change the subject.

"To our friends, old and new, thanks for making time to come and hang with us on the West Side this Friday night—the traffic must have been crazy."

Everybody raised their glass, and Louis chimed in boisterously, "Yes, Shabbat Shalom!"

Everyone laughed and said, "Cheers."

Immediately, my heart stopped beating. My mouth went dry. I looked around the table. Everything was in slow motion until my eyes met JB's. He shook his head, discreetly yet adamantly, as if to say, *Don't say it. Just let it go.*

But I couldn't. In the chaos and frenzy of preparing the perfect meal—something that I couldn't even eat—I had forgotten who I was serving the food to: *my guests*, in other words. Louis's colleague was a Conservative Jew, as was his wife. They had only just recently been Orthodox, and had switched to Conservatism after their marriage. *I knew this.* We had had a long conversation about this at their house a couple of weeks ago. And now this lovely woman was mere inches away from tasting my delicious beef bourguignon, whose second main ingredient was *BACON*.

I watched as the spoon came closer to her mouth. A myriad of options screamed through my head, and just as the spoon touched her lips, I screamed, *"STOP!"*

The entire table sat upright, apparently startled.

"I . . . I'm so sorry. But you can't eat that," I whispered, holding back tears. "I made a mistake."

As I cleared plates, I explained the terrible oversight I had made, and the couple were very, very gracious about it—and relieved I had let them know. I told them I would whip something up quickly in the kitchen and ran back to see how I could fix this. Louis followed me in, and I collapsed into tears. I had let everyone down—most important, him. He tried to calm me down and tell me that it didn't matter.

A couple of minutes later we emerged from the kitchen with a new plan: as Louis announced we would be having salad pizza, I was already pouring the rosé.

POP *Truth:*

YOU CAN'T HAVE IT ALL, AND WHY WOULD YOU WANT TO?

+ Nobody cares that you can do it all.

+ Figure out how to get that shit off your plate.

+ Don't even with the guilt over outsourcing.

The evening I just described worked out fine, but that's not the point. The point is this never should have happened in the first place. Sure, I'm a decent cook—it was a big part of what I did at LEAF. And that's the point. Cooking was work to me. Just because I could do it and was good at it didn't mean I was obliged to do it *for fun*. I am certainly no Ina Garten. Cooking isn't my life. I love food, and cooking is a great way to get to that food. But it's not the only way.

On top of that, I didn't need to be at Whole Foods at peak hours, shopping for a crazy long list of items. I didn't need to be in that parking lot, fighting my way out. If I was going to cook, I could have easily Instacarted the order and avoided all the chaos—allowing more time for myself.

Finally, because of my need to impress and do it all, I forgot the real reason we were getting together in the first place—to forge new relationships. And in my attempt to do everything perfectly, I had overlooked a very fundamental aspect of any good dinner party: *the people*. Even if I hadn't had this colossal fail, when I look back on it, except for the forty-five minutes where I was being praised, I was totally stressed out and miserable. I had forgotten me, the most important person there. In preparation for the dinner party and for 80 percent of the evening, I had suffered, beaten myself up, exhausted myself (even more than I already was), stressed myself out, and for what? I realized that the best time that evening was when we all snacked on pizza and drank wine and had a good laugh. I was relaxed, not pulled in a million directions, and could enjoy our company. And of course, as soon as I relaxed, our guests could, too.

The following morning, I vowed to start outsourcing what I didn't really need, because trying to do it all was (a) counterproductive and (b) ultimately very unfulfilling. If doing it all means you're not enjoying yourself or the experiences you're having, there truly is no point.

IF IT'S NOT BIG 3, IT GOES

Well, sort of.

Establishing concrete goals for yourself makes achieving them a lot easier. That sounds stupidly obvious, right? But working hard without clear goals is what so many of us do. It's like our insane efforts are a huge fishing net that we're casting and hoping that surely some awesome things will get caught in it, right? Maybe. But what's more likely is that you'll also spend an enormous amount of energy on things that you don't really care about. And we're done with that. In chapter 5 we set our goals and we're going to move toward them with ease and energy. Except . . . there is still that report to file to your boss, dishes in the sink, and your best friend's birthday party to plan.

In order to truly commit to your three choices, you will need to let go of a lot of activities and actions that don't support those choices and are, in fact, holding you back. You'll have to be ruthless in deciding how to use your time. The first step in creating an outsourcing system that works for you is acknowledging that (a) you don't have to do everything in order for it to get done and (b) it's okay to ask for help or to pay someone else to do certain jobs. This can be a very tough transition for an overachiever/control freak (looking at myself here!). Give yourself some time to get used to the idea. Actually, there are a few ideas you'll have to get used to.

1. You can't do it all.

2. You shouldn't try to do it all.

3. Other people will do things differently than you might and that's okay.

4. You aren't a bad wife, girlfriend, mother, daughter, employee, etc., if you don't keep doing everything you've done so far.

5. Everyone will get over it. Seriously.

When you start the process of outsourcing or delegating chores and tasks, it can feel like you're being lazy or that you're passing the buck onto someone else. And for an overachiever that's an unfamiliar and uncomfortable feeling, but it's absolutely not the case. You're not shrugging off responsibility, you're clearing the way so that you're able to place your focus where it belongs: on work, activities, and, above all, time that moves you into alignment with your Big 3 choices.

But first you have to actually know what that looks like. Is your day full of the small steps that will take you toward your goals? Or are you maxed out on activities that don't support your goals at all, leaving you to squeeze in goal-supporting activities here and there when you're already wiped out? Guess which is the right way to go? Not to worry if you suspect that your current schedule is far from ideal. I'm going to hook you up with a whole bunch of ways to clear your time.

SEVEN-DAY TIME-TRACK CHALLENGE

Time is the wisest counselor of all.
—PERICLES

The challenge here is to simply make note of how you spend your time. You don't have to make an effort of any kind, other than to be accurate. You'll be breaking your days into one-hour increments and making notes on how you spent your time. At the end of each day, while it's still fresh in your mind, make a few quick notes that describe how you spent your time, how you felt, and whether each task you completed supported any of your goals. You can use a small notebook or a spreadsheet on your computer—whatever makes it easy for you to keep an accurate accounting of your time. Remember, this is not a reason to beat yourself up—we're expecting that your day and your goals aren't in perfect alignment yet.

Here's how a day might look. Let's say this person—shall we call her Julie?—has decided to become the manager of her team at work, to run a half marathon, and to make more time for her friends as her Big 3 goals this year.

7 A.M. Alarm goes off. Hit snooze three times and run out of time for a pre-work run. Feel kind of bad, as I'm trying to work out four times a week. Big 3: 0

8 A.M. No time for breakfast. Get dressed and fly out the door. Grab a coffee on the way into work. Anxious about getting a proposal ready for a new project. Big 3: 0

9 A.M. Get pulled into marketing meeting for a project I'm not on. Annoyed. Feeling behind already. Big 3: 0

10 A.M. Finally at my desk. Work until lunch on the proposal. Feeling better, more in control. Big 3: 1

12:30 P.M. Lunch out with my work wife. A very good gossip sesh. Big 3: 1

2 P.M. Called into my manager's office to discuss new interns starting tomorrow. She's asking if I can take over their orientation. Said yes, meant no freaking way. Big 3: (can't decide if this is a pass or fail, to be honest)

3 P.M. Email around trying to find out how to orient the stupid interns. Big 3: (see above)

4:30 P.M. Spent the past hour at work catching up on expenses. Should have done this last week. Big 3: 0

5:30 P.M. Conference call with the Seattle office. Do they understand time zones? Frustrated that it meant I'd miss yoga class I thought I'd catch. Big 3: 0

6:00 P.M. Stop at the grocery store on the way home. So hungry that I buy some pretty terrible things. Argh. Big 3: 0

7:00 P.M. Went for a run. Added an extra mile to my usual route and felt amazing. Big 3: 1

7:30 P.M. Realize my roommate has not emptied out the dishwasher—again—and have to spend twenty minutes tidying up the kitchen before I can make dinner. Kind of pissed. Big 3: 0

8:00 P.M. Made a quick dinner at home, thought about spending the night with Netflix but instead had a hot bath and got into bed early with a book. Big 3: 1

As you can see, Julie had as many misses as she did hits in her day. At first glance, some of the misses look like things she can't control: getting pulled into a meeting that doesn't involve her, being asked by her boss to pick up an office chore, needing to stop for groceries, her roommate's messiness. But honestly, could she do away with some of these issues? Ah, yeah. (And she should also go back and read chapter 3 again, too.) Because she was pulled into tasks and chores that don't support her goals, you can bet that this day was not a fulfilling one. You can feel her frustration rising with each task that pulls her off course. In fact, that sense of frustration or lack of control is the very feeling you should be paying attention to when you do this exercise. It tells you that (a) you're not doing something that supports your goals and (b) you should be trying, if possible, to outsource it. This frustration is something that accumulates and on its own starts gnawing away at your day-to-day productivity. Pay attention.

ANOTHER REASON TO TRACK

Adding an interesting twist to your new habit of time tracking comes from Laura Vanderkam. Vanderkam is an author, researcher, wife, and mother of four, and still seeks self-improvement enough to also write for the *New York Times*. Recently, I read her fascinating article "The Busy Person's Lies." She spent an entire leap year tracking how she spent her 8,784 hours to gain perspective on where her busy hours were going. At the end of the year and her experiment, what Vanderkam found surprised her.

Her results showed an average of seven hours–plus of sleep a night, multiple massages, solo beach days, and 327 hours of leisurely (not self-improvement) reading. In similar studies, she found that "professionals tend to overestimate work hours; we remember our busiest weeks as typical."

Initially, I was comforted by these findings—okay, so we aren't too busy, *we just think we are!* But that relief lasted a quick minute, because when you think about it, what do these findings really mean? Sure, we have the time to do stuff that isn't work-related—physically—but if we have no real recollection or emotional response to these great moments of pause or "me time," then what are they really worth? Are we really making them count? I mean, if a tree falls in a forest and no one hears it . . .

So tracking allows us to see where we're spending our time, even if we aren't always feeling where we're spending our time. But it also drives us to be mindful of when we're on the right path, timewise, and when we're blindly hacking through that forest. The fact of the matter is, even when it comes to what you're doing for relaxation, you've got to make it count, or why bother? E.g., if you're hanging out with your friends but you're totally distracted by your Instagram feed, does that really count? No. If you're getting a massage but all you're thinking about is how much you need to get done on Monday, does that really count? No. So as much as you're analyzing whether you're spending your work hours productively, so too should you be analyzing whether you're spending your play hours productively. The whole system must work in harmony.

WHAT STAYS AND WHAT GOES?

Once you've finished your seven-day challenge, it will be crystal clear where your time is moving you toward your goals, or at least building a foundation for them, and where your time is pulling you further away from your goals. Our first order of business is to get rid of as many tasks as possible that don't move your forward. We'll work through a few ways to do just that. But it won't always be possible, or even desirable. You may not be in a position—yet—to quit your job and start your own business. The window of possible choices for you is narrower . . . for now. But you can still use the freedom you have to obtain maximum results. And even if you're in a situation where you're working at a job you don't love but must stick with temporarily, keeping a time log likely highlighted some opportunities for you.

Another essential principle is value. As in, what are your values? Spending time with your kids may not be one of your Big 3 choices because you're already doing it. So keeping track of your time may show that you hang out with your kids after school and help them with their homework. That window of time could be put toward studying for your GMAT, but if family time is what you value, then that window isn't open for you.

Do what's possible. Don't waste time with guilt.

PLAY TO YOUR STRENGTHS

In evaluating ourselves, we tend to be long on our
weaknesses and short on our strengths.
—CRAIG D. LOUNSBROUGH

What are you amazing at? Are you great with numbers and do you get energized by making budgets work? Then it's probably a skill that will move you toward one of your Big 3 goals. People will come to know you for this talent, you'll be asked to utilize it, you'll get better at it, and it will continue to snowball in the right direction. But nobody's perfect, so for every skill that comes naturally there's something we dislike and struggle with. Does making presentations leave you uncomfortable or even a little queasy? Your reluctance to be in front of a roomful of people is likely obvious to everyone. Because you're not great at it, people don't respond to what you're communicating. You can sense that, and it all goes downhill. And that's okay!

In an ideal world, you should focus on what you do better than anyone and what you love to do more than anything else, because that's the value you can bring to any situation. It's a value you bring to work, to relationships, and to yourself. I spoke to the CEO of the amazing health site *Well+Good*, Alexia Brue, about how she decides what jobs she'll keep for herself and what she outsources. As much as her decisions are ruled by what's reasonable for the lead of a fast-growing digital brand, it also comes down to how she wants to use her time.

"I have a six-year-old and an eight-year-old and they're in school all day. So our amazing nanny, who's been with us for over six years, has time during the day. I don't have to grocery shop or cook or even think about what the kids are having for dinner. Without her, I wouldn't be able to get as much done as I do. I try to spend as much time as I can with my kids and I don't want that to be grocery shopping and cooking. And cooking is not something that really relaxes me. It's not something I enjoy. That's what makes it all work."

Of course, Alexia could force herself into the kitchen to answer a societal expectation that a mother should be making her kids' dinners. But what do you think her kids prefer? A stressed-out mom who is busy in the kitchen at the end of the day or a chilled-out mom who is able to sit down and enjoy a meal with them, giving them her full attention? For some people, a half hour in the kitchen is the perfect way to unwind, but if it's not, there's no point in feeling guilty about it.

DO THE OUTSOURCING MATH

Do what you do best, and outsource the rest.
—PETER DRUCKER

When you can't decide if a task or chore should be outsourced or if it's easier just to do it yourself, analyze the cost versus the benefits of the situation. You might feel a bit guilty paying for an Uber to take you back and forth (maybe $35) to a work event, but you're saving $10 in parking and the thirty uninterrupted minutes you'll get in the back seat of that car might be used for (a) answering work emails, (b) listening to a podcast you've been looking forward to, or (c) looking out the window and letting your mind wander. There's no right or wrong choice, but just realize that you have a choice.

It's possible to feel that paying a cleaning service $60 to give your place a once-over every month is a waste of money, but if you really hate doing the deep cleaning and having someone else do it buys you a free afternoon, then it may be well worth it. But maybe it's cathartic for you to blast tunes and get your home gleaming.

Take a minute to think of what you'll gain and lose by each choice. Do a cost-benefit analysis. Do you make up the amount of money spent in time, found energy, or productive minutes? There is no right or wrong answer, but you must do the math to make the intelligent choice for you.

OUTSOURCING TAKES PRACTICE

Like any new skills, delegating and outsourcing take practice. Using technology to get things off your plate—ordering groceries online, shopping a website for the bikini you'll need for your vacation next week—is the simplest form of outsourcing. Having an actual human do things for you is a horse of another color. Jane Francisco, editorial director for the lifestyle group at publisher Hearst, talks about her experience working with an assistant when she became editor in chief at *Chatelaine* magazine. "I learned about outsourcing from my assistant, Sue, the first time I met with her to talk about the job. She came with the job. I was talking to her about her experience and who she'd worked with. Prior to my predecessor, she'd always worked for men. So I said to her, 'Interesting, how do you feel about working for women versus men?' And she said, 'Oh, I'd way rather work for men.' I asked her why she found it to be better and she said, 'Because the men actually treat me like a partner and they literally turn everything over to me. They don't try to micromanage me and they let me do everything. With women, they want to support me.' And I thought, *I get it*. You're worried about asking for another person to do something."

Even when it's that person's job, it can be a learning curve for women to ask someone else to assist them and then allow them to actually do it. Jane recounts all the things Sue said she did for her male employers. "She told me, 'The men I worked for asked me to do everything from buy gifts for their wives to go to events with them. It made me enjoy my job more, and I felt like I was in charge of something and I felt trusted.' So I don't think I did as good a job as the men in her life, but I said, 'Okay, I'm going to try this. I'm going to try to let you be in charge of me that way.'"

Allowing her assistant to look after the tasks she was skilled at—managing schedules, handling expenses, answering emails—allowed Jane to focus her energy where it belonged, on the pages of the magazine.

How to Outsource or Delegate Like a Boss (Even If You Aren't One)

1. Don't apologize for asking for help or for giving someone else a task.

2. Don't expect people to do things as you have done them or would do them. Did it get done? By someone who isn't you? You're good.

3. Give clear instructions and expectations. You can't imagine a job is going to be completed if it's not clear what the job is. Don't hope that your roommate will one day empty the dishwasher without you asking. Ask her.

4. Get out of the way. Don't hover as a person does the project or task you've asked them to do.

5. Don't take a job back—right away—if it gets screwed up the first time. People need a chance to learn. Don't use other people's mistakes as a reason you have to do it yourself.

6. Say thank you.

What Not to Outsource

1. Things you love

2. Things you're best at

3. Things that must be done exactly as you want them done

APPS, ONLINE SERVICES, IRL HELP

The following list provides a short but not exclusive list of different apps that are available to quickly (and often for free!) help you manage your lifestyle. Like all things tech related, some will be around for a long time, and some might have gone under by the time this book goes to print! But the idea here is that the internet is full of resources just like these are just one Google search away from helping you out. Browse the list below for ideas, or start your own search if you're looking for something really specific.

Home

TaskRabbit: For home repairs, small moves, drop-off or pickup of anything

Angie's List: Resource for certified handymen/women, construction professionals

AmazonFresh, Grocery Gateway: Delivery for the things you buy every week

UberEATS: Meals for when you're too busy to cook

Blue Apron: Delivery service of DIY meals—you are provided with the ingredients and recipes, you do the cooking

Instacart: Local food delivery from Whole Foods and Erewhon (some markets only)

Shyp: Pickup/drop-off service for anything needing to go to the post office, FedEx, UPS

Upwork: List of freelancers who can help you get personal stuff done

Shop Fetch: App that allows you to enter in your shopping list and that will source and buy the cheapest options

Handy: Connects you with professionals who will clean your home or perform such tasks as assembling furniture or mounting a television

OurHome: Fun, reward-based app for delegating household chores

ChoreMonster: Award-winning chore delegation app

DRIVING AND PARKING

Waze: Traffic navigation app

ParkMe: Quickest way to find a parking spot

Uber, Lyft: Personalized car services—often less expensive than a taxi—that can also be used for delivery of documents, etc.

FAMILY

Zum: Child ride service or day care

Care.com: Babysitting service

UrbanSitter: Babysitting service

SittingAround: A co-op of parents who trade babysitting services

eNannySource: Nanny service

ORGANIZATION

IFTTT: All-in-one app that connects hundreds of other apps all in one place (e.g., Instagram, Google Drive, health apps)

Pocket: For organizing all the things you find in the moment that you want to read/check out later

Things: An award-winning task manager that helps you achieve your goals

24me: It's like having your own personal assistant. It handles all your organizing, scheduling, bill paying, and more

Evernote: An incredible way to capture and organize your work, in order to have all your info in one place. It's also built with integrated share features, making collaboration on projects very easy

Unroll.Me: The best way to clean up the clutter in your in-box. This app lines up all your "subscription" emails and allows you to easily delete anything that isn't serving you at the moment

WORK

TeuxDeux: Straightforward to-do app

Wunderlist: For those who like to cross things off a list

DocuSign, HelloSign: For dealing with documents digitally

Freelancer, Fiverr: Virtual assistants, transcription, marketing, email newsletter creation, etc.

GOALS

Rooster: Reading tailored to your taste and schedule

TripIt: Organize travel

Audible: Listen to books anytime, anywhere

GTFO Flights: Last-minute flight deals

HotelTonight: Last-minute hotel deals

Matchbook: Remember the places you loved eating at and want to try

Salt: Bookmark and share restaurants and cafés

Litsy: A place to share and discover your favorite books with your favorite people

NON-APP-RELATED OUTSOURCING

Some things you will want to do a deeper dive on and won't feel comfortable simply signing up for an app. (Everyone has different sensitivities.) But some things that are probably worth a conversation and a little cost-benefit analysis are the following:

Child care

Housecleaner

Handypeople

Tutors

Personal chef (to do weekly meal prep)

DELEGATING

At the end of the day, knowledge is power, so the more you know about how you're spending your day—where you flow with ease and where you get caught up—the better prepared you'll be to start letting go of the right stuff. As you've heard me say many times at this point, even if we could do it all, *we shouldn't*. Why? That would make for a busy life, not a productive one. Freeing up your schedule so you can spend time on the things you really enjoy and move forward toward your Big 3 by letting go of stuff that can be done reasonably by others is what starts to effortlessly propel you in the right direction. In other words, I'll take a slice of salad pizza and a great laugh with friends anytime over the perfectly cooked meal that I can't even eat.

Here's the Drill

- ❐ Seven-Day Time-Track Challenge: Note how you're spending your time, hour by hour, for one week. Be sure to pay attention to how you're feeling and whether the way you spend time is supporting your Big 3 goals.

- ❐ What are the tasks that make you feel most stretched?

- ❐ What are the jobs you intend on outsourcing? Make a note about how you'll get these items off your list. Kiss them goodbye!

CHAPTER SEVEN

How to Use Your Time Much Better Than You Are Right Now

Venice, spring 2009: *The British are coming!*

As I did most every morning at this time in my life, I was sitting at my desk, in front of my old desktop computer, refreshing my emails to see if I had received any feedback or notes on my latest script. After a series of near hits but ultimate misses, I had vowed this would be my last script if something didn't pop. I was confident, however, that after all the work I had put into it, and the incredible response I had received thus far, this script was *the one*. As I looked at a stack of dog-eared "intent to foreclose" papers for the four walls that were currently keeping me warm, this *needed* to be the one.

My writing partner, Larissa, and I had caught a lucky break seven months earlier, when we'd sent an advance copy out to a couple of colleagues for their initial thoughts. At the last minute, I'd realized I hadn't sent it to any women for their opinions, and it dawned on me that that was a mistake. I had a reference from a friend of a female

British producer who was doing some big stuff after partnering with a very successful British TV director. Both were repped by the biggest talent agency in Los Angeles. I emailed the producer and asked if she would read my script and give me her thoughts before it went out.

She agreed, and to my great shock, she emailed me two days later, full of praise, asking if I'd shown the script to anyone else. When I told her we hadn't, she asked if she could show it to her directing partner and her agent. *I was elated.*

Less than a week later, both had read the script and all three seemed very excited. She asked that I not show the script to anyone else. She wanted exclusivity and wanted to work with me on the story to get it in shape in order to meet with her director. For the next three months we went back and forth—there were a litany of notes and changes. It was a ton of work, but the process was exhilarating. Finally, the script was in fighting form, and the director had read the latest version and wanted to meet.

A meeting was arranged in my small Venice backhouse. We sat around my small, rickety "dining room" table and talked shop. The director walked into my tiny abode while sipping a beer, plopped down, and promptly kicked his feet up on the table. His arrogance was unfathomable. I was shocked but chose to ignore his actions in order to keep things positive. We got to work. He loved the story but wanted still more changes. This time they were even more involved—adding in a new character, etc. While I was very happy to have him sitting in my house, discussing the project, I was disappointed we were still discussing changes to the script rather than a deal. What's more, I was going to have to convey this news to my writing partner, whose frustration with the process was mounting.

Regardless, I agreed to make the changes and got to work. Over the next couple of months the producer was back in London on a project, and so our correspondence became a little fragmented. *It was just the distance*, I thought to myself. When I became insistent on some feedback on my latest round of edits, she assured me she would be back shortly to finalize everything. And that's what brought me to that morning in the spring of 2009, compulsively checking my emails.

A light, gray rain had begun to fall as I stepped away from my desk, still in my bathrobe, to fetch a second cup of coffee. The hum of my old coffee machine crescendoed, nearly masking the familiar chime of my computer alerting me to an email, followed only moments later by the buzz announcing the arrival of a text message on my cell phone. I swirled in some milk and sugar, then headed back to my desk, grabbing my phone on the way. As I dropped back down in front of my computer, I read a text from Larissa.

Call me ASAP when you read my email.

A lightning bolt of excitement shot through me. *This was the moment we'd been waiting for.* I spun around in my chair and clicked open my emails.

I had one new email, forwarded to me from Larissa.

As I scrolled through the email searching for the words *would like to officially make you an offer* . . . I became more and more confused. What was I looking at? There was a script or a least part of a script attached. My writing partner was also an actress, and she'd attached what are called "sides," which are small portions of a script that actors learn for auditions. A note from Larissa's agent at the top of the email explained which scenes she would be reading for and where she was to show up.

I texted her back, irritated: I don't get it? What is this??

Did you read it??? READ IT!!

I clicked back on the email, reread the body—no new information there—then hesitantly clicked on the sides attached. I began to read, then stopped about halfway down, my heart racing with every new stanza. I stared at the pages in disbelief. Quickly, I shuffled back and forth to the top, back down to the bottom, and then back again. My mind was reeling.

It was a version of our script! Where had this come from? How could she have been sent a time to audition for it?

What the fuck was happening?

As I searched for clues, I discovered in small type at the bottom of the script's title page, A *project produced by* and *to be directed by*.

Of course, it was produced by the British producer and directed by the British director.

I still don't understand how I managed to stay upright for the next ten minutes as I pieced together what had happened. When the dust settled, the cold reality was this: not only had our script been stolen and not only was it now, apparently, set to be made—but for the past three to four months I had been doing their rewrites for them, for somebody else to use. (We must have done a great job; it went on to run for five seasons!)

My heart was completely broken.

As I commiserated with my writing partner, I alternated between waves of rage and despair. We discussed our options. *Which were few, with our resources.*

After we hung up, I sat at my desk, totally despondent, wondering how the hell I had gotten here. I really had nothing. All my hopes and dreams were tied up in this last, big chance and now I had no direction whatsoever, and very few options.

How the story ends is how you'd expect it to end: Goliath beat David.

POP *Truth:*

YOU CAN'T CONTROL TIME, ONLY PRIORITIES.

✦ Use your time so time doesn't use you.

✦ Create your perfect productive day.

✦ Blast through crap you hate doing.

The end of that story really is not the point. It's the *"how did I get here?"* that matters.

I had my one goal: to make a living as a writer. Now, as we learned from chapter 5, one goal is not enough, and this story is a perfect example of that. There was no balance in my life—nothing to offset this one goal. Being happy, successful, productive, or fulfilled was a zero-sum, all-or-nothing game. A game that I lost.

Within that one goal, there were a couple of very important lessons to be learned. The first of which was, in order to be successful as a writer, you can't have a story that only has a beginning and an end. The middle is as important as either. In other words, my two objectives were: write a script, sell a script—with no thought as to how A and B would connect. How they ultimately did connect was an all-encompassing, totally consuming life takeover for close to a year. In the end, though an incredible script was the final product, all my resources were depleted and the process had been totally inefficient. It allowed me to do nothing else. There was no balance. No room for creating other life opportunities—and as a result, failure was not an option.

The only thing is, failure is always an option—as I found out the hard way.

In retrospect, what I should have done was spend as much time on my process development as I did on my character development. And by process I mean time management. I should have organized my days and weeks with a clear schedule that allowed for a more complete life, creating more personal opportunities for growth and using the time that I had set aside to write in the most efficient way. And I should have used my free time to reinvigorate myself rather than just running myself ragged on a single-lane highway.

I'd allowed two things to happen during the course of that year. I focused on only one goal, meaning that when it got knocked out from under me I had nothing else to keep me standing. The second thing I did was let time run me, rather than run my time myself. I had no time to live a more balanced life—one that might lead to other opportunities, let alone refresh me—because I hadn't made the time. I felt I had no choice but to pour every second into this script, but of course I could have made other choices.

It's why I'm emphatic that the choices you make in your Big 3 be wide-ranging. Choosing to focus on different arenas not only creates a more symmetrical life, it also allows each of your goals to fuel the others. Imagine the energy circuit created by the day I'm about to describe. Getting up early to fit in a run for that half-marathon you're training for clears your head as well as lets you start your day feeling like a superhero. Knowing you've got a date to look forward to in the evening makes getting through building an elaborate PowerPoint presentation less arduous in the day. A night out with your guy or gal gets your mind off work.

And of course, putting energy into yourself as a professional and an athlete means you don't need your romantic relationship to fulfill all your needs.

In this way, when failure threatens to tiptoe toward your door, (a) you've got two feet firmly planted and are much more prepared to fight and (b) you can't lose everything, no matter what happens, because of the process you've put in place for yourself. It's timeless and invaluable, easily transported from project to project, better with each use, leading to a holistic use of your time. Such a system creates energy and a more complete sense of self. In short, acting blindly just trying to get through something or to the end of something is a sure way to fail and exhaust—regardless of your talent or desire.

Secondly, if you are waiting, *and I mean for anything or anybody*, you are doing something wrong. If you have time to refresh your email thirty times to see if the producer—who is ultimately stealing a script behind your back—has hit you up with a deal, you are not using your time productively. Waiting is an energy killer and a spirit killer, and with every minute you wait you are losing your own personal power. Luckily, it's easy to create a day for yourself where waiting on other people isn't necessary. When you take the time to prepare a rigorous weekly and daily plan—which should involve as many massages, meditation sessions, or long walks as you see fit—it allows you to build indestructible productive muscle memory. Once this muscle memory is in place, it will become second nature, like breathing. People who employ these types of methods never find themselves waiting for answers or outcomes, because they're already working on the next things that are keeping them vibrant and fully charged.

As when adopting any new habit, creating systems around time management will seem at first to take more time. It's why many people avoid them. It's a natural reaction: you're sold on the idea of using your time more efficiently, you give it a try, and you feel like you're getting less done than ever. I get it. But seriously, the heavy lifting of getting started will pay off in a big way once you get going. Making time to set goals and a schedule will quickly become second nature, and you'll see how much more you can get done, without overdoing and overstressing.

Much of this book has been about asking you to let your heart and mind run wild and dare to go big with your dreams. You've looked inside to uncover your most authentic desires and gotten real about what your future focus will be. Knowing and articulating goals is crucial to manifesting them. If your goals are the heart of your new approach to life, then organization is the skeleton. Without a structure for your time, your goals can easily get lost in the chaos of a busy life. But the right structure will pour gasoline on those goals. I'm going to share with you the very best ways to get the most out of your days, from how to structure a productive day (even if it's filled with things you're not so thrilled about) to avoiding the dreaded procrastination. These power moves can be applied to anything you want to get done.

SMART SCHEDULE

The key is not to prioritize what's on your schedule, but to schedule your priorities.
—STEPHEN COVEY

Before I even describe an ideal day for productivity, I can already hear some of you piping up with, "But I'm a night owl, this isn't going to work for me! Inspiration never strikes until at least midnight." I hear you, but guess what, hush up. Real talk: guess who aren't night owls? High achievers. Guess who doesn't wait for inspiration to strike? The highly successful person. Multiple studies have shown that high achievers tend to follow certain patterns. One of the most important patterns in these people's lives is that they get up and get going early. According to research, the first two and a half to four hours of the day are when our brains are sharpest. Don't waste that time on meetings, emails, or breaking down last night's episode of *The Bachelor* with your cubicle mate.

1 *Intentional mornings.* To mimic top performers, don't just set an early alarm: you need to also set your mood. There's been a lot of talk recently about morning rituals, and many leaders rely on them. Studies show that feeling happy allows us to get more done and work more creatively. Whether you exercise first thing or meditate before jumping in the shower, committing to a routine that *you know* will put you in a positive state of mind matters. Whatever your path to feeling positive is, do it every day so it becomes nonnegotiable, like brushing your teeth.

2 *First things first.* Tackle your top priority first. This seems so obvious, but many of us are in the habit of blowing through some easy, mindless work to ease into the day. Few things are as motivating as progress,

so crossing off your big-ticket item on your to-do list will boost your whole day. As well, self-control diminishes as the day rolls along, meaning you're more likely to avoid a challenging task later on.

3 *You've got mail.* Don't check emails first thing. Answering emails is by definition a reactive task and we want your mornings to be proactive. I'm not going to lie: this is an extremely tough rule to follow at first. What if it's the job offer you've been waiting anxiously for? Or your ex, realizing he was a damn fool? But it's probably not those things, right? In fact, you know what most of your emails are before you even look at your phone. Gap jeans are 40 percent off, *again*. Your mom has a hilarious joke to share with you. And the rest can really wait. It's just not worth it to get wrapped up in what other people want you to do in those important couple of hours in the morning.

4 *Avoid people.* Seriously. Particularly for people who work in offices, distractions are everywhere. If you can find a quiet spot, like an underused boardroom, grab it for those critical first hours of the day. If you can't, then use other, not-so-subtle hints to get people to leave you alone. Put on headphones, even if you're not listening to anything. If you've got a side hustle, get up even earlier and dedicate an hour to it before you head in to work.

5 *P.M. meetings.* Use the later—and less sharp—part of the day for meetings, emails, and other busywork, if possible. Not all of us have the freedom to shape the course of our workdays, but if you do have that freedom, take advantage of it. And you may have more input than you imagine. Share the concept of only-afternoon meetings with your boss and she might like the idea of a more productive team.

6 *Make a list.* End your workday by writing down goals for the next day. This is a powerful tool for turning off and enjoying your evening. Once the next day's list is down on paper, you no longer have to worry about it. Use your time off to boost your well-being—hang out with friends, get outside, exercise—rather than just zoning out online or in front of the TV. Having a list of priorities already decided on when you start your day means less friction and procrastination.

7 *Get to bed.* Giving yourself a bedtime is a radical act of adult behavior. Science is not having it with your "I don't need more than five hours" nonsense. Lack of sleep leads to lack of productivity. End stop.

To see how your day lines up against this ideal, try tracking yourself for a few days. Apps like RescueTime allow you to see, at least in the digital world, how you spend your day. Are you in that Word doc, writing your novel for the ten hours a day it feels like, or are you succumbing to the siren call of Instagram for fifteen minutes of every hour? There are many apps out there that can help you get an accurate look at your time as well as help you shape it, in the form of reminders and blocking troublesome websites.

LOOKING AHEAD MEANS NO WAITING

Nothing's going to come to you by you sitting
around and waiting for it.
—ZOE KAZAN

In the story I shared at the top of this chapter, I fell into a common trap of allowing my time to be ruled by someone else. I was waiting for someone else to give me the green light to move forward, and I let myself get paralyzed by the waiting. Of course, many of your goals are going to require input from other people and won't always guarantee an automatic response. That's why it's vital to have a schedule that allows you to leapfrog over things you're waiting on to tasks you can pick up on your own.

One of the greatest drags on productivity is starting. The inertia we all feel at the beginning of anything, whether it's researching an article or drafting a business plan, is real. It's the biggest piece of friction we can feel in our days. Once the wheels are turning, the flow of moving forward is much smoother. Even if you get off to a shaky start, you've started, and you've got something to work with.

No matter how all-encompassing a project is, you can't give everything to it. By breaking that work into pieces in your schedule, you can also make time for looking forward. This isn't the same as multitasking. You'll be working on your main project when you're scheduled to. When you're done with that, you'll take a break. Then you'll look ahead to something that will exist next. Make a few notes, make a few calls. Get something started, if only in the smallest way. Setting up this kind of pause to look ahead means that if your main project gets stalled due to forces beyond your control, you've got something to turn your attention to. And it's something that has already begun, so you can jump over that tricky, gritty, getting-started feeling. Most important, pausing frequently to assess your progress helps you develop your sense of control of your time.

WHO YOU ARE DICTATES HOW YOU SPEND YOUR TIME

When things are easy for you, you almost don't need to schedule them at all. If you love to move, then working out a flow for the new yoga class you're teaching will be the thing you can't wait to do in the morning. What you may have trouble getting to is the backend work the website for your yoga studio requires. If one of your Big 3 goals is to open the doors to your studio in six months, you're going to need to attack both. But how you use your time for each of these tasks can be quite different. Don't get me wrong, you have to create a schedule for your days, regardless of how you're filling them, but your approach can change. For activities and jobs you're naturally drawn to, you can block off longer periods of time and feel confident that the time will be well spent. Tasks you feel repelled by or daunted by should always be broken up into smaller pieces and be scheduled into manageable, smaller blocks. Working with your own **P** for personality is key to not getting discouraged. Be kind to yourself by making challenging jobs as easy as possible.

Be clear with yourself about the different reactions you have to work you have to get done. Pay attention to your reactions to the work you do. Notice where you get stuck in your day.

The items you do easily and with enthusiasm are your flow activities. They can afford to live in the afternoons, or wherever you may have less energy. The fun these tasks deliver can override the 3 p.m. slump. The tasks you feel more resistance to, or even repulsion toward, are more challenging and require more support—which is coming your way.

MICRO GOALS

The reason blue-sky dreams can seem out of reach is their size. You want to have the biggest beauty YouTube channel. You want to become a neurosurgeon. You want to open your own restaurant. You can imagine how it would feel to be on the peak of that hill where your vision lives. But it's so far away from your current, not-so-dreamy life that it feels impossible. So we give up before we even get started.

Not so fast. No one just *becomes* a YouTube star or a neurosurgeon. They take a step toward their goal. Then another. Then another. Meet your new best friend: the micro goal. These are the bite-size pieces of action that you're going to build all the way to you doing exactly what you want to do. Breaking a challenge into smaller, more manageable pieces achieves two key things: it allows you to focus on one thing at a time (crucial for productivity!) and it allows you to get to a win sooner. But perhaps most important, it allows you to get beyond feeling overwhelmed and into action. You'll know that you've broken down a big goal into micro goals when you can enter the little pieces into your calendar. Micro goals are a way of understanding how to get from here to waaaaay over there, but they're also a way of managing time.

Here's how it works. Let's take something you need to accomplish to get to one of your Big 3 choices, say, launching a lifestyle website. The big task in front of you might be finding a designer to work with. How are you going to find one you like? Whom you can afford? How will you convince a great person to work on your site? Do you feel like having a nap right now? It's okay, take a deep breath. We're going to break this way down.

Micro Goals for Hiring a Web Designer

1. Make a list of friends who have websites.

2. Write an email asking those friends for recommendations. Ask them to share with you, if they will, what they spent on designing their sites.

3. Create an inspiration board on Pinterest.

4. Write a single sentence that describes how you'd like your site to look.

5. Create a document where you list all the functions you want your site to have.

6. Write a job posting for a designer.

7. Look at sites like Upwork and Freelancer and check the work of designers.

8. Decide on a deadline to have the names of three designers to approach and put it in your calendar.

9. Look at the portfolios of designers that your friends have recommended or that you've found on freelance platforms.

10. Contact three designers.

11. Send each designer a description of the site of your dreams as well as some visual references.

12. If possible, book face-to-face meetings.

13. Ask for a quote and a schedule from the designers you like.

14. Decide on a designer.

15. Call the designer and hire them.

It's important to be as specific as possible when you're creating a to-do list of micro goals. If you're including a task that isn't a single action, then you know you can break it down further. While the idea of finding a designer was daunting, most of these little jobs are not. You're working toward your goal, building a sense of accomplishment, and above all, you're not freaking out or giving up. Whenever a hurdle feels too high, there are usually ways to break it into small, actionable pieces. None of these tasks takes more than ten or fifteen minutes, but you do need to schedule them.

As you work through a list of micro goals, it's important to strike each one off as you move along so you know exactly where you are in the process. You'll gain a sense of accomplishment and momentum if things are moving along. And what if they aren't? If you're struggling with a step, ask yourself if it needs to be broken down further. Do you need to ask for help? Do you need to do it at all? Take note of the kind of task that doesn't come easily to you. It may require the productivity-sprint approach.

PRODUCTIVITY SPRINTS

You've heard of HIIT, right? High-intensity interval training is all the rage in fitness right now. Short, full-on bursts of activity are alternated with short resting periods, and the results leave those associated with steady exercise in the dust. Not only do you burn more calories using HIIT, you continue to burn more well after you've changed out of your running shoes. The appeal of HIIT is obvious: who wouldn't want to get more out of less time spent working out?

The same thinking can be applied to work, in the form of productivity sprints. These short, measured, and highly focused sets are an ideal way to attack challenging items on your to-do list. They don't suit every activity. When you're about to dive into an activity that you naturally excel at, you don't need productivity sprints—you'll be in flow state in no time and will easily get a lot done. But for those items you have anxiety over, avoid, or stress over, they're perfect. They sharpen your mind, they break work into small pieces, and they build a sense of accomplishment. Productivity sprints are perfect for handling your expenses, writing a difficult email, or tidying a messy room.

I'm going to teach you how to supercharge your productivity without adding hours to your already long-enough day.

1 *Decide what you're working on.* Create a to-do list, but one that's not too long. Writing a novel-length list is only going to leave you feeling like you failed.

2 *Do one thing and one thing only.* The key to productivity sprints is a single focus. No matter what we may tell ourselves, multitasking is a myth and one that leads us to feel exhausted and defeated. Our brains can do one job at a time, and every time we flick from one task to another (or, say, from writing a script, then jumping onto Facebook for a few seconds), we lose momentum, or what psychologists call flow (when we're completely engaged in an activity, we're both relaxed and energized). If you work on a computer, this means while you're doing focused work, you don't have email, Twitter, or Facebook open. Clear your desk of everything except the work you're tackling.

3 *Set a timer.* How long we're best able to focus on a single task is up for debate. In creating his well-known Pomodoro Technique, Francesco Cirillo used a tomato-shaped kitchen timer to track twenty-five minutes of concentrated work, followed by a five-minute break. Research performed by DeskTime, a time-tracking app, shows that fifty-two minutes of work followed by

a seventeen-minute break may be an ideal schedule for productivity. There probably isn't a one-size-fits-all answer to the perfect work-break balance. In my opinion, half an hour of work followed by a five-minute break is just about perfect. It's enough time to move forward with a project but not too long that I'm daunted to start. Whatever you choose, set a timer and break when it's time to break. Knowing a break is coming has been shown by a study out of Cornell University to make you use your work time more efficiently.

4 *Get up and move.* Exercise is important for our physical, mental, and emotional health, but did you know it also makes us smarter? A short burst of exercise will boost your mood, but it also increases your ability to work once you're back at it. A study out of the University of Illinois showed that kids who took a brisk walk were better able to focus afterward than kids who didn't move. Likely you're not keen to get sweaty in the middle of your workday, but don't make this a leisurely stroll. It's great if you can step outside and get some fresh air, but indoor walks deliver the same mental benefits.

5 *Keep track.* As you're cycling through your productivity sprints, make note of what you're striking off your to-do list. You always want to build momentum, and feeling like you're succeeding is powerfully motivating.

HOW NOT TO SPRINT

You can't grind all day. Well, you can and many of you likely do, but we're not on the road to burnout anymore, remember? Choose a few key tasks—three to five—you want to accomplish each day and be sure that they feed into one of your Big 3 choices. You don't want to use your most focused energy on projects that don't require it. It may be more appealing to start your day by booking flights for your best friend's bachelorette in Vegas, but you can easily do that while watching TV tonight. You also don't need to sprint on activities that come easily and naturally to you. If you love writing, there's no need to stop every twenty minutes. You might lose yourself in writing a blog post or a letter and be at your desk in a focused way for an hour. Sprinting is hard work and takes practice, so you want to use it on the challenges that need you at your most badass self.

YOU WANT ME TO SCHEDULE WHAT?

When you think of the things you have to put in your calendar, it's usually the things you can't forget (a meeting with a client, or your nephew's bar mitzvah), might easily forget (teeth cleaning), or are looking forward to (vacation!). But what about the aspects of your life that are key to your well-being and may even feed into some of your Big 3 goals? Such as exercise, time with friends, and even sex?

In this work-obsessed era we're living in, we place an enormous value on professional, paid, career-building work. We put an increasing amount of time toward those goals. And even if some of our Big 3 goals exist outside of the professional realm, we force those goals to be squeezed into the sliver of time we have left after work. Sometimes we get to them, but many times we don't. It's this misshapen schedule that is largely responsible for our sense of dissatisfaction and, ultimately, burnout. In order to build a full, balanced life, we need to tip the scales in favor of the goals outside of work. And that means making a commitment to them by blocking out time on our calendars.

Because we favor professional work and treat our "free time" like an afterthought that only deserves a seat at the kids' table, it can feel awkward shifting that balance. Even activities that don't relate to your goals may be essential to your well-being. Making time for them is an important way to remind yourself of your own importance. Taking charge of this shift is going to immediately increase your sense of control in your life. You're no longer at the mercy of your schedule—you're setting it!

1 *Decide when your workday should end.* Some of us can't control when our workday starts and finishes, but to the degree that you can, you should. Resist the impulse to be the last person in the office as a way of making professional points. Knowing the day ends at five thirty sharpens your productivity during the day, and gives you something to look forward to.

2 *Decide what you want each week to include.* What nonwork activities either feed into your Big 3 or rejuvenate you in a way that feels essential? Having a hard time thinking of what to include? Think of

the last time you were out with your best friends, laughed until you cried, and wondered why it had been so long since you got together. *That's* the sort of item we're looking for on this list. Exercise, social time with close friends, dinner with your family, sex with your partner, time spent in nature, reading?

3 *Decide how often you can make time for these essentials.* Can you fit in a girls' night once a week? Can you run three times a week? Would sex two or three times a week bring you and your partner closer together?

4 *Decide to make these priorities clear to yourself by putting them on your calendar.* Things that are scheduled have a higher chance of actually happening. Hoping to get to Pilates class is not the same as putting it on your schedule for 6:30 (meaning you've got to leave the damn office!).

5 *Decide to make these priorities clear to the people involved in them.* It's all well and good to tell the people in your life that they matter, but nothing speaks like action. Showing up for people lets them know they matter to you.

Here's the Drill

- ❏ **Pro tip:** Use an online app for a week to get an accurate look at how you're really spending your time. Two great apps to get you started tracking your time:

  - ❏ **RescueTime:** Track how you spend all your time online.

  - ❏ **Hours:** This is a great time-tracking app for freelancers and small businesses.

- ❏ Make a list of the three tasks you most look forward to. These are your flow tasks.

- ❏ Make a list of the three tasks you wish you could avoid. These are your sprint tasks.

- ❏ List three to five nonwork items you're going to add to your weekly schedule that will improve your life balance (e.g., sex, a walk, reading, a bath, brunch with friends).

- ❏ Create an ideal schedule in which each day includes an aspect of each of your Big 3 goals.

CHAPTER EIGHT

Assemble Your POP Posse: Mentors, Allies, and More

Santa Monica, 2010: *Windburn*

On a particularly blustery afternoon in February, Geri (my fledgling business partner) and I stood at the corner of Ocean and Wilshire, our laptops tucked under our arms. Blinded by the harsh, cold sun, battered by the vicious wind whipping off the Pacific, we were at a standstill, not sure what to do next. The only thing we knew for sure was that this beating we were taking from these (unusual) L.A. elements felt like a very strong metaphor for something. And that something wasn't good. Now, with hair flying everywhere, eyes watering from the sting of salt air, shoulders hunched, we were a mere shadow of the two put-together, heads-held-high young women who had entered the tall glass tower not a mere half hour before.

You see, this was our last investor meeting, and it had gone pretty much like all of those before it. In short, it was a pass. But more than a pass, it was a condescending pat on the head, from people who "loved the concept" but weren't sure that the two women who created the concept had what it took to run the business.

Rewind eight months. I had recently been hired to run marketing for another start-up within the fashion industry. I quickly had to make a couple of key hires and was referred to Geri Hirsch. She was the founder of a small but very well-respected fashion blog, *Because Im Addicted*, and at the time was working in marketing for a much-buzzed-about social awareness start-up. Instantly upon meeting we connected and it wasn't long before we were sharing a desk at our new jobs, enthusiastically spitballing creative social ideas and marketing campaigns for our new CEO. Unfortunately, within a few short months it became apparent to us that the weight of financial burdens and the flailing infrastructure that had sunk so many other start-ups before it wouldn't be improving anytime soon. This shiny new opportunity was not what we had signed up for. What did have incredible fortitude, however, was our budding relationship. We both were running successful blogs on the side, we had a ton of personal opportunities being pitched to us, and beyond that we were both working after hours on new web ideas that we hoped to turn into million-dollar businesses. We were two peas in a shitty start-up pod.

One afternoon, after a particularly grating group meeting where the all-male executive staff were pitching us on ideas for a "cool" women's social shopping experience—all ideas in direct contrast to the concepts we had presented the week before—we stepped out on the promenade for a Pinkberry. We were both seething, but Geri was excited to tell me about an opportunity that had come her way. She had been given the chance to pitch the business idea that she had been working on—a lifestyle destination for the millennial woman—to Condé Nast, which was looking for ways to cross-pollinate all their different magazine audiences. The meeting was set for two weeks from then and she asked me if I had any interest in joining forces with her. *"We have got to get out of here!"* she exclaimed. She didn't have to ask me twice.

For the next couple of weeks, we worked diligently on evenings and weekends, getting our plan and presentation together. After we finally presented, we were met with a very, very enthusiastic response—and though our model wasn't the perfect fit for Condé, we knew by their reaction that we were onto something. We were going to try to take LEAF—living, eating, and fashion—to the next level.

For the next couple of months we gave it everything we had, burning both ends of the candle, working our full-time jobs during the day, creating new video content for LEAF on the weekends, and trying to play catch-up with our blogs every evening. It was a lot, but we were fully energized. As we blindly created content, hoping to get noticed, we finally stumbled upon our ticket. Barneys New York, the prestigious retailer, had seen our videos on Geri's blog and loved them. They asked us to create a three-part series with them, using, for the first time ever, shoppable technology—meaning you could actually shop the clothes *through* the video.

We created the flagship videos, and they were an unbridled success, with the content we produced selling six figures' worth of clothes. We had our proof of concept—now we just had to go sell it.

Immediately, as we worked on our pitch deck and shared our plans with the people around us, what surprised me was that so many people who had had such great enthusiasm before were now a little pessimistic about our chances. And more and more, I felt we were on the receiving end of cautionary tales of people "with a lot more experience than you" failing. When this was just a hobby we were cute and inspiring: now that we wanted to make a real go of it, we were naïve and foolhardy. The "I-told-you-so's" were just waiting to pounce. Undeterred, we put our heads down and worked until we had something we felt good about—and more important, until the people we sought advice from felt good, too. We had definitely made some compromises regarding our plans, based on said advice, but all in all, we felt the strategy was cohesive and compelling. Next, we set out to sell.

Between the two of us, we had quite a few contacts in the VC, or venture capital, and incubator worlds, and we started booking pitch meetings.

After nearly three months of pitching we had nothing. There seemed to be a cumulative excitement over the idea but less enthusiasm for our ability to execute, and with each meeting our confidence was being further chipped away.

Cut back to that blustery afternoon in Santa Monica. As we stood on the corner, we both were thinking what neither of us wanted to say—LEAF was dead. We had just had our last investor meeting and there were no bites. With heavy hearts and even heavier footsteps we walked back to our desolate office, resigning ourselves to our fate.

A couple of days later, we received an email from a young digital agent at a major L.A. talent agency. She had heard about the project, but more than the project, she was interested in us. She wanted to meet. With nothing to lose, we gladly accepted. The following week we sat down to chat, and what happened in that meeting was incredible. We showed her our pitch deck, and instead of picking it apart, looking for ways to destroy it (as had happened at all the other pitch meetings), she first let us talk out our vision. She began writing notes, tracking the parts in which our real enthusiasm came through. Then, based on that we went through the deck and she noted the same thing. After we were done, we talked about why the things that didn't excite us were in the deck at all.

Frankly, we had never looked at it from that point of view. After further reflection, we realized that most of those points were elements that we had added to the deck based on different people's advice along the way (an act of trying to appease all of those who had helped), and as a result, the pitch read as a sort of patchwork quilt rather than a finely oiled machine that truly represented our value proposition.

We left that meeting with homework and a new lilt in our step. Our excitement was not only renewed, but perhaps surpassed even our initial zeal. This idea of focusing as much on ourselves as on the idea itself when working on the pitch was a light-bulb moment. What's more, this agent decided we needed some serious, positive mentorship— so she sent out a couple of emails and within a week we were working with two more successful women, from very different areas of the market, who were just as enthusiastic. Geri and I reworked the entire pitch, with their guidance and support, rebuilding not only our concept but our confidence in both the idea and ourselves. It was a truly magical time. So when we set out for our second go at fund-raising, instead of the blustery gusts that had greeted us after our first failed attempt, this time we had the wind at our heels.

In retrospect, it isn't surprising at all that a mere two weeks after we'd jumped back into the fire we had our first offer, which would later turn into our first deal and a $900,000 check. LEAF was very, very much alive. We now had the ability to leave our full-time, dead-end jobs and dedicate 100 percent of our time to our dream.

I can safely say that without the solid mentorship of this small group of incredible women—who didn't provide us with answers, but created the right climate of support for us to be able to perform at our highest level and have our most creative ideas revealed—LEAF just might have died right there on that windy corner in Santa Monica. Surrounding ourselves with the right people made all the difference in the world.

POP *Truth:*

THE PEOPLE AROUND YOU WILL AFFECT YOU LIKE NOTHING ELSE, SO CHOOSE THEM WISELY.

✦ Are your relationships helping or hindering you?

✦ How do you cut out toxic relationships?

✦ How do you build an all-star crew?

There's an old saying that says you are the average of the five people you spend the most time with. I'm not prepared to think of myself as average, and you shouldn't look at yourself that way either, but I take the point. The people we surround ourselves with have a major impact on our lives—from our emotions to our health and, of course, our productivity. As much as I've been encouraging you to embrace your own goals and to listen to your opinions first, it's essential that you acknowledge the power of the people around you. The truth is, some people lift you up and some people drain you. And in the same way that I've asked you to stop allowing distractions to slow you down, I'm asking you to look at the people around you and see if you have people in your life who are holding you back. If you think of your personal community as an ecosystem, is yours a supportive ecosystem that allows you to flourish, or are there toxic corners that leave you feeling like shit?

Right now we're going to look at creating a posse—a POP posse—made up of allies and mentors who will help you meet your goals. It's going to mean taking a hard look at the people around you, potentially distancing yourself from some and getting closer to others. You may realize that you need to cultivate new relationships in order to cast your dream team. Now, to be clear, I'm not talking about analyzing every relationship you have. The fondness you feel for your cousin Bobby, a complete slacker who's never going to help you with a damn thing, can remain unchanged. What we're looking at is the network you need to meet your Big 3 goals.

Of course, you can be productive in an environment where you're not supported by those around you. We all know stories of people overcoming this kind of obstacle. But it's not easy. And why not put yourself in the best possible position to succeed? Not having a positive environment has real consequences in regard to your ability to reach your goals. In fact, a study at the UK's University of Warwick found that unhappy employees were 10 percent less productive than happy ones. Research in brain science shows us that humans are more focused and creative—as they need to be, to be their most productive—when we feel positive. We can problem-solve more easily and get burned out less.

The people you're close to tell the world a lot about you, but more important, they tell *you* what you're worth. It feels simple enough to be common sense. If we just meet and I tell you most of my friends are unemployed and that my family would rather stay home than travel, you're going to make some assumptions about me. You'll probably see me as someone without a lot of life experience or the ambition to get it. But if we're introduced and I describe my friends as leaders in their fields, you're likely to assume I'm on a similar track.

And there's a good chance you'd be right. Humans are mirroring machines. Several years ago, the covers of women's magazines were emblazoned with headlines warning that your friends might make you fat. You won't be surprised to hear the truth is just a little more complicated than that. The researchers Nicholas Christakis and James Fowler relied on a long-term, wide-range research conducted by the National Heart Institute to look at how the people around us play into our emotional and physical health.

EMOTIONAL CONTAGION

We think of emotions as being something particular to us. And to some degree they are. You experience your feelings personally. But emotions also exist in context of our communities. Each group, whether it's a group of friends or workmates, or even a social media network, has an emotional tenor that affects us. You would expect that the moods of your spouse or best friend would impact you, but the ripples that happiness can cause may be several friends-of-friends removed. In a fascinating piece of their research, Christakis and Fowler looked at how happiness—and unhappiness—move through groups. Looking at large groups, they saw clear patterns where a person's happiness was closely related to the happiness of those around them and that each happy friend you have increases your likeliness of being happy. Not so surprisingly, happy people tended to be in the center of friendship groups.

They also looked at how happiness or unhappiness could ripple through social media. The researchers looked at a very simple metric: smiling in images posted on social media. The smilers tend to be the hub of social groups, with non-smilers existing on the periphery.

BEHAVIORAL CONTAGION

While emotional contagion might feel somewhat obvious—of course being around a friend wearing a storm cloud for a mood might affect yours—behavioral contagion is a stranger seeming thing. Christakis and Fowler found that behaviors like smoking, drinking, and over-eating to the point of obesity are also highly contagious (hence those manipulative headlines). Having a friend become obese makes you 57 percent more likely to become obese yourself. You're 36 percent more likely to become a smoker if you have a friend who smokes. And drinking is contagious, too. Christakis and Fowler propose that the way people behave around you can act as a kind of permission. If you're out for lunch with a friend who decides to indulge in dessert, even if she doesn't urge you to join her, you're likely to give yourself the okay to order a brownie, too. As humans, we're constantly calibrating what normal is, and the people we surround ourselves with are a vivid part of that picture.

Each emotion and behavior seems to come with its own idiosyncrasies. Weight loss or gain is most often transmitted between men and men and women and women. When it comes to what's normal for our bodies, we're obviously more likely to compare ourselves to others of our own gender. Happiness or unhappiness is more easily spread among friends than among workmates. Crazy question: Does a woman's place in the world make her more susceptible to emotional contagion? Who said yes? The researchers Hatfield, Cacioppo, and Rapson have found that women tend to be more vulnerable to emotional contagion since we're raised to be more emotionally attentive.

WHO CARES?

Some of the feelings and habits you can "catch" from your community are positive. If someone in your Facebook feed starts a thirty-day running challenge, it could inspire you to dust off your sneakers and get moving, too. Sadly, sometimes it's the most negative of vibes that are the easiest to pass along. But before you can start deciding who deserves a position in your POP posse and who doesn't, you have to make another, bigger decision: *that you matter*. It's easy to walk through life meeting the people you meet, maintaining friendships you've always had, spending time with people you happen to work with . . . in other words, not making conscious choices about the people you spend time with. But when you think about the effect other people can have on your energy, your well-being, and your ability to meet your own goals, that approach doesn't make sense. You have to believe that you're worthy of a fantastic network in order to get one.

My business partner Geri considers her personal community on her blog, *Because Im Addicted*, one of the most important factors in her own happiness. "I'm really extremely conscious of it. I think about toxins in, on, and around your body, and trying to eliminate toxicity in your life around your body. In my opinion, it's not just the chemicals that you're spraying in your home or the air that you're breathing, but it's the relationships that you're surrounded by. In a lot of ways, I see that those are more toxic, because they mentally take so much away from you, if you're in an abusive or just a low relationship. And I think it's okay to step back from friendships or whatever the relationship may be and take a pause, take a break, and circle back to it."

It may feel uncomfortable to analyze the value of people in your life. But making the call that a so-called friend is bringing you down with her constant negativity doesn't make you a selfish person, it makes you someone with self-respect. It's critical that you remind yourself that your well-being is worth protecting and cultivating. And of course, any relationship worth anything is a two-way street. When you have connections that bring out the best in you, you're able to be your best for your friends and colleagues, too. If you have toxic people around you, it's natural to become guarded and withdrawn. When you're surrounded by positive and encouraging peeps, you're able to give that positivity right back to them. Again, one of my key indicators for who should stay and who should go is taking a close look at my energy levels in the presence of different people. Do I feel charged up and ready to go or drained after specific encounters? Often energy is the best source of information in these cases, as the emotions of "assessing" your friends can often be distracting.

SEVEN TOXIC PEOPLE TO WATCH OUT FOR

You can find toxic people anywhere, sadly. You might sit next to one at work, have a long-standing frenemy relationship with one, or, worst of all, have one in your family. You know you have a toxic person in your life because you'll often feel drained after spending time with them. You feel anxious around them and worry about their moods. Sometimes you even find yourself mirroring their behavior. To sum up: these people are poison. Luckily, though, they're pretty easy to spot.

THE EMOTIONAL BULLY

You never know what you're going to get with this person. One day she's cracking jokes and listening with interest to your stories about your weekend. But the next day she's a black cloud in a dress. You wonder if you've done something to offend her. Pretty soon you realize you're walking on eggshells during every encounter.

THE VICTIM

Victims are tricky. You're likely to feel sorry for them at first and be drawn into their troubles. You'll want to be helpful and supportive. But you soon realize that nothing is ever this person's responsibility. The world is unfair to the victim and if you're going to have a relationship with this person you have to be prepared for the constant support they need. Plus, it's only a matter of time before they feel victimized by you.

THE JUDGE

This person's weapon of choice is their disdain. They move through life like an eye-roll emoji. Every idea put forward is dumb, no plan being created will ever work. Don't expect this person to offer their own suggestions. She's not a risk taker and she doesn't want you to be either.

THE ENVIER

This person is a scorekeeper and things are never in their favor enough. In this person's world, there isn't enough to go around. You won't see this person cheering a friend or colleague's success—they're too busy wondering why they didn't get that promotion or opportunity.

THE PASSIVE-AGGRESSIVE TYPE

This can be a tricky person to get a handle on. Passive-aggressives use emotions subtly to control others. If you're working on a project with this person and her idea doesn't get chosen, rather than move on or express disappointment, she will quietly stew, and then resist progress through being late to meetings or misplacing materials. If you ask her what's wrong, she'll say, "Nothing," but you'll continue to feel her low-level anger.

THE GOSSIP

At first, the gossip can be a fun friend or workmate. They seem to know everything about everyone and, let's be honest, who doesn't like to have the inside scoop? But it doesn't take long to realize this person takes a little too much pleasure in the misfortune of others. How long until it's your shortcomings being dissected?

THE PESSIMIST

This person complains. A lot. But they express their negativity and para-noia with such confidence you can start to ask yourself if you're seeing things clearly. Maybe your boss *is* trying to undermine everyone on staff.

HOW TO AVOID TOXIC PEOPLE

Even if you choose your allies carefully, you're still going to have to move through the world. There's a limit to the control you can have of the people you'll be dealing with on any given day. And sometimes that will mean dealing with highly negative or toxic people. However, it's possible to interact and even work with a toxic person and not be drawn into their cyclone of negativity. But it takes awareness and emotional maturity to spot these people and to disengage from their games. The emotional-intelligence people at TalentSmart studied more than a million people to find that 90 percent of top performers are skilled at managing their emotions in times of stress. Identifying toxic people and being able to stay calm and in control in their presence was a heightened ability in this group.

1 *The first step in managing toxic people is to pay attention to your own reactions.* Does someone make you uncomfortable or anxious? Do you worry inordinately if a particular person is upset with you? Ask yourself what's going on. Take the time to examine a situation on its face. If you generally feel good about yourself but there's a person in your life who brings out your insecurities, pay attention!

2 *When you find yourself in the proximity of a toxic person, be purposeful in your thinking.* Remaining mindful in the face of a manipulator takes a concerted effort.

Try making a note to yourself even if it feels a bit goofy. *Okay, Vivian is trying to get me to trash-talk our boss and I'm feeling super uncomfortable. It's not the way I want to operate at work so I'm going to change the subject and if that doesn't work, I'll make up an excuse to remove myself from this situation.* You don't have to explain your discomfort with this person. In fact, the less you discuss emotions, the better.

3 *Don't go along just to get along.*
Many toxic people continue their obnoxious behavior simply because they can. The office gossip always has plenty of ears, the victim plays on everyone's sympathy. But you won't be lured into harmful patterns if you refuse to play the role you're being handed. It's easy just to laugh a little uncomfortably when a passive-aggressive person zings us. "Wow, not everyone can wear *those* colors together. Interesting!" says your passive-aggressive neighbor as you're leaving your apartment. Rather than take this backhanded compliment, you can call her on her rudeness. "I'm pretty sure that means you're not a fan, but that's okay. I really dress for myself."

4 *Learn to disengage.* Once you know someone to be a toxic element, you need no longer be affected by their behavior. Rather than being pulled into the drama these kinds of people create, set boundaries for yourself. If your sister makes snarky comments about your apartment, remind yourself it's about her, not you. If you start looking at toxicity as almost a handicap, you can move from feeling victimized to rising above and feeling some empathy.

THREE NOT-TOXIC BUT NOT-GREAT PEOPLE TO KEEP AN EYE ON

The people just described are fairly simple to identify, if you're being honest with yourself, because of how they make you feel. Even if it's not easy to avoid them, some part of you will feel repelled by them. But there are many relationships that exist in a gray area in human relationships that can be much trickier to navigate. Developing as a person means changing. Hopefully we all grow in confidence, experience, and perspective as time and life go on. And not everyone in your life will be growing at the same pace, or growing at all. It's no one's fault, but your relationship with someone you used to be completely simpatico with may suddenly feel . . . well, awkward.

PUT-DOWN PARTNERS

Less dangerous, but far more common than the toxic person, is the self-deprecator. You know this person because it may be you. She groans over the morning coffee run, "I'm such an idiot, I should have gone to bed at a decent time to be ready for my presentation but instead I watched the whole season of *The Crown.*" Or she shares a shot of her kid on his way to school in a pirate costume. #LaundryDay. #MomFail. Of course, some of these put-downs are for laughs. Studies show that when high-status men put themselves down, it's seen as charming. Because, you know, what's he got to lose? But as women we actually have a lot to lose. Particularly in the professional arena, where women can struggle to receive the respect they deserve, people may be taking your funny jokes about yourself at face value. The other side of this habit is that it implicitly demands to be rejected. When someone puts herself down, even as a joke, the required response is "No! You're a great mom!"

Amy Schumer spoofed this habit in her hilarious video "I'm So Bad." A group of women are having dinner in a restaurant, taking turns finding ways to call themselves bad. One woman recounts a recent evening where she polished off a birthday cake on her own. "I was like, that's enough, pig, I'm so bad!" Her friends come to her aid immediately. "You are not! Your thigh gap, like, is the envy of every thigh gap!"

Rx: The first way to shut down the put-down habit is to notice it. Are you doing it? Does someone close to you do it? If you realize you're the culprit, work on weeding insults out of your vocabulary. No more "I'm so lame" before launching into an anecdote. If you spend time with someone who has this habit—such as a colleague—try your best not to mirror the behavior. And if it's a close friend, you may need to get explicit. You can bring it up by talking about yourself, not by critiquing her. "I've noticed I do this thing where I put myself down and I really don't want to. I'm going to be trying to drop it from my vocabulary. Maybe you could help me by pointing it out when I slip up?" You've put it out there in a way that doesn't judge your pal.

BAD-HABIT BUDDIES

You were inseparable in college. Fries for lunch and a pint of ice cream in front of the TV was a daily ritual. And weekends meant shots until you had to help each other stagger home. Through the miracle of a youthful metabolism, you made it through this phase and have nothing but happy memories. Now you're more about that green-juice life but your friend still wants to party like you're living in the dorm. You've tried suggesting meeting for yoga and brunch but she's not having it. "Come *ooooon*," she'll say, "let's go out and have fun!" And you're stuck with either slipping back into old patterns or feeling like a wet blanket.

Rx: Again, if this is someone you care about, you're going to have to spell it out. Let your friend know that you've embraced a new regimen and you'd love her help with it. People respond better to requests for support than they do to complaints. In other words: more carrot, less stick. You could tell your friend, "I'm really busting my ass to get my new website going and I can't afford to lose days to feeling hungover anymore. I don't want to see you any less. Can we switch our Thursday night out to an early dinner so Grandma can get to bed at a reasonable time?"

THE FRIENDSHIP MIRAGE

Making big changes like a move to a new city, starting a new career, or getting married can send ripples through all your relationships. Once you come up for air from these kind of life shifts, you may be surprised that everyone who was there before either isn't or shouldn't be. With a little time and distance it's possible to see that what looked like a friendship was just time spent in close proximity. Maybe that colleague you had lunch with every day for two years was good company but now that you've moved on to a new job you're just not missing a closeness with her, because it was never really there.

Rx: I admit it, this one is tough. You might get lucky and the other half of the mirage feels as you do, and you ease into the birthday-note-on-Facebook kind of zone. But if the person you're leaving behind doesn't understand why you're not as connected as you used to be, it's a bit trickier. There are few road maps for a friendship breakup. You can maintain boundaries that feel appropriate to you without ghosting your old pal. Explain that your new job or relationship or project is taking up more time than it used to and make a suggestion that works for you. If you feel like seeing this person once every six months is appropriate, then stick to it. Politely and kindly, of course! She'll get the message that things have changed. She may not want to remain friends, but at least you will have been clear.

YOUR PEOPLE

Now that you've got your antenna up for people you need to avoid, how do you attract the people who are going to support you and bring out the best in you? Remember, we're talking about the people you need around you to help you achieve your Big 3. You're going to want to connect with people who, in addition to being generally awesome, get you and what you're trying to achieve. If you're planning on opening your own restaurant, you'd be crazy not to get to know people who have been in that business.

1 *Be yourself.* The best way to make an authentic connection with someone is to stop second-guessing and adjusting yourself to fit in. Say what you mean. Yes, you're going to turn some people off. And that's the point! When you behave authentically, you attract people who appreciate you. So what if you repel people who don't think you're hilarious, smart, and fascinating? Those are the people you want to walk on by. The more you do this, the easier it gets.

2 *Pay attention to how you feel.* If you're practicing mindfulness, this will be easier. Take

note when a conversation makes you light up. Notice when ideas flow effortlessly between you and another person.

3 *Be intentional.* Often we approach dating or finding a partner with a nearly professional focus. And why not? Our romantic lives are important and who we partner with has a huge impact on us. So why not think of your POP posse in the same way? Think consciously about what you need in your inner circle. Do you need a cheerleader, someone who challenges you in a supportive way, a coach? (Answer: all of the above.)

4 *Be the energy you'd like to attract.* It's no good wishing you had an A team of smart, positive, supportive people surrounding you while walking around like the end is near. If you want amazing people in your life, you have to be amazing in their lives, so be sure to create reciprocal relationships. Stay engaged with what's going on in your A team's lives. Cheer for their victories, commiserate when they fail, but really be there.

HOW TO FIND A MENTOR

One of the key players on your team should be a mentor. Or mentors, if you're lucky. Because this person is knowledgeable, experienced, and willing to share their expertise, they are extremely valuable and should be treated that way. It takes work to find and cultivate a relationship with a mentor, but the benefits are well worth it. A mentor is like having a coach for your dreams.

Jewel Burks is the genius behind Partpic, a visual search app that allows you to take a picture of bolts, screws, and what have you, and then search for and purchase them. Jewel had been working for Google as entrepreneur-in-residence. Her job was to help business owners—particularly those who are black, Latino, and female—use Google products to boost their start-ups. But she missed her hometown of Atlanta and eventually moved back. She was working at a parts distribution company and coincidentally was struggling to help her grandfather find a part for his tractor. With this aha moment she was inspired. She raised $1.5 million, put a small team together, and created Partpic.

Given her experience within a major company and her own start-up, Jewel is often asked to speak at conferences and by journalists (or book authors!) on issues of diversity. While the digital world may represent an enormous opportunity for those historically barred from success (such as women and people of color), diversity has still been the Achilles' heel of the capital that tech requires. It's why Jewel is so passionate about the role mentors have played in her life and how women can use them in theirs. It's important to have people in your life who believe you can fulfill your dreams. "Mentors have played a huge role in my life, and in my career," Jewel told me. "It started from a young age. It started with my mom." Her mother's own insurance agency is having its twentieth anniversary this year. "I remember being a little girl and watching her get started, watching her be so dedicated to getting everything off the ground, serving her customers, working weekends, and really sacrificing a lot. That was my early exposure to the idea of entrepreneurship."

With that early example to guide her, it's not surprising that Jewel recognized the value in having experienced women on her side. While attending Howard University, Jewel met Marie Johns, a trustee at Howard. The former deputy administrator of the U.S. Small Business Administration took Jewel under her wing and showed her the ropes in D.C. Stacy Brown-Philpot, now the CEO of TaskRabbit, was instrumental in Jewel's move to Google while Brown-Philpot was at the tech giant. "At various stages of my life, I've had amazing exposure to incredible women in particular, and men, too, but I think I've been able to connect with some powerhouse women who have demonstrated that success is possible and given me the idea that I could pretty much do whatever I want."

If you're not lucky enough to cross paths with people who inspire you—and particularly if you're looking to change industries this could be the case—you can still hook up with your own rock star mentor. But, again, be prepared to be purposeful about it. Since Jewel has had so much experience in this arena, I asked her what her process is if she wants to make a connection with a high achiever. These are her tips:

1   *Do your homework.* If you come across someone via an article they've written or you've heard them speak at a conference and they inspire you with what

they've got to say, go the extra mile and check out more of their work. Have they written books or given a TED Talk you can watch on YouTube?

2 *Make the next move.* Says Jewel, "If I see that they're speaking at a conference, I'll attend the conference. I'll attend their session and sit in the front row so they realize I'm interested in getting to know them. I'll introduce myself and ask for their contact information." Remember, these are people who are putting themselves out there as public personalities. They're expecting to be approached in this way.

3 *Follow up.* Don't be afraid to send an email asking for a get-together.

4 *But don't just take.* You've got to bring something to the table yourself, not just be about what you can get from this person. "Try and make it so it's mutually beneficial, more than just, 'Hey, I want to pick your brain!' but more like, 'There's an article that's interesting because it relates to your industry and I'd like to share it with you.'" Or offer to help them in whatever way you can. If they see that you're super helpful, they'll be willing to share with you, too.

5 *Be prepared.* Go into a meeting with a potential mentor with a specific question or challenge. Now that Jewel is on the receiving end of this kind of request, she knows even more about what makes these sessions productive. "I love it when people say, 'I'd love to spend some time with you and this is what I want to cover.' That shows me you've thought about this and it shows me you're serious. You're not just throwing it out there and hoping for the best."

PEERS

Having someone in your life whom you look up to, admire, and hope to be like eventually is powerful. But it's not the only way to build a support system for yourself. When Jaclyn Johnson, the incredible force behind millennial-women-focused professional conferences Create & Cultivate, was getting her business off the ground, she realized that someone even just a little bit older than she is wouldn't relate to her issues. "I have close friends who are really successful, like Steph Korey and Jen Rubio from Away luggage. We were all starting out at the same time and we were able to come together. We'd say to each other, 'This is what I'm doing, what are you doing? Who are you hiring? Do you know this kind of person?' It really is where the help is. I need to know what to do right now, right in that second. I needed that younger connection. I feel like younger entrepreneurs are all in the same boat. We all need this stuff right now."

That community approach has guided Jaclyn's vision for Create &

Cultivate, where young female entrepreneurs can share what they're learning, pick up new skills, and network with like-minded women. Jaclyn's experience with what powerful assets the people around you can be has been a key to driving her business.

Here's the Drill

While I was writing this chapter, I was amazed at the amount of information and study done around the importance of those you keep close. More than any other chapter, this topic seemed to have the most to say as far as research goes. While that surprised me initially, after thinking about it, it makes total sense. As I hark back to my earlier analogy (raising money for LEAF), our success was directly related to changing the company we kept, and that made all the difference. And as a result, the exercise section of this chapter is one of the most robust.

When you start this exercise, you're excused if you feel a little, well, gross. I'm not asking you to make a who-goes-and-who-stays list. Yet. What I'm asking you to do is to think seriously about your days and who you spend time with. Go through a week's worth of days in your mind. Some people might appear regularly but have little effect on you (like the barista at your local coffee shop) and some may appear very infrequently but have a large impact (the yoga teacher you see once a week who gives you a megadose of calm each time). Also, keep in mind people you might not see in person but have regular contact with—say, your mom, whom you make a weekly call to. Consider whether someone significant is missing because of travel or some other kind of change to your usual flow.

☐ Create a list of the people who exist in your life over the course of a week.

☐ Beside each name write down how you feel when you're with them, whether it's excited, anxious, or competitive.

☐ Then make a note of a value you share with each person. Don't worry if some of the values you're tracking don't seem profound. If you and the woman at the next cubicle at work only share a sense of humor, but she's otherwise a pleasant acquaintance, that's fine. With the childhood friend you met at sleepaway camp and have remained close with you'd expect to have a longer, more detailed list, including things like loyalty, a sense of adventure, and honesty.

A caveat: if you're realizing you have negative feelings about someone close to you because of a particular situation—an unresolved argument, an unspoken disappointment—can you imagine resolving it with an honest conversation? This exercise isn't about weeding out *any* bad feelings, but about establishing how you feel about your key relationships *most* of the time.

☐ Now I want you to imagine you've received some good news. *Really* good news. Like, huge-promotion, got-engaged, landed-a-book-deal kind of news. You're vibrating with excitement, it's so amazing! Who are the people you call first, and why? Do you call your dad because you know he'll have the best reaction? Is it the friend who's going to scream like the news is her own? Is it your boyfriend, who'll be popping champagne before you even finish filling him in?

☐ Write down the names of the people you want to call with the great news.

☐ Now, who do you dread telling your news to? Is there someone who is prone to jealousy and whom you'll need to downplay your happiness with?

☐ Who do you not want to call with good news?

☐ Scientists use Venn diagrams to show how two sets overlap. Put the people most regularly in your life in one circle and your cheerleaders in another. Where they overlap is Team You. Or at least, that's the ideal. And that's what you're aiming for: that the people most often in your life and your space would be those most supportive of you. If they're not, then you've got some changes to make. You may find that the people who are most often in your life—and having a constant impact on your emotions and behaviors—are not the ones who fill you with energy and well-being.

☐ If you've never had a mentor before, you might not know what to look for in such a person. Start by thinking of what you wish you knew. How to lead a team? How to raise money? How to negotiate for a raise? Make a list of the skills and qualities you'd like to learn from a mentor. Keep this list in mind as you move through life. It will help you spot potential mentors.

CHAPTER NINE

How to Create Your Own
Personalized POP Plan

I may have spent most of this book encouraging you to cut your
to-do list in half and then in half again, but that doesn't mean I don't
understand the satisfying nature of a list. It feels damn good to strike
things off your list—it's like nailing a strike in bowling. Psychologists
have long observed that the human brain is soothed by the creation of
to-do lists. It diminishes anxiety, establishes a structure, and allows you
to see what you've accomplished. The key, as we've discussed, is to have
reasonable, balanced expectations for what you can and should try to
get done each day, each month, each year.

An equally fascinating, but complicating, element of our relationship to lists is what's called the "Zeigarnik effect." Developed by the
Russian psychologist Bluma Zeigarnik, it describes our tendency to
focus on what needs to be done and forget what has been done. It was
based on an observation of waiters at work. They could only remember

orders that had not yet been served. Once they had delivered a customer's food, the waiters could no longer remember who had ordered which item. There was no longer a need for that information, so the brain deleted it. Think of it as the brain's way of saving space.

The downside to this important brain function is we easily forget to give ourselves credit for our myriad accomplishments. A list or a journal that outlines how we spend our time is important in advance of work to create structure, but also essential to look back on. Seeing what you've been able to do builds a sense of accomplishment (if you're able to do what you've set out to do) and can act as a cautionary note (for things you seem to not be able to manage). In reviewing your day by looking back on your list, you're performing a kind of mindfulness that helps you stay on track. And even if you aren't ticking off items, that's valuable also. If something keeps reappearing on your list because you can't seem to get it done, that tells you something. You either need to break that task down into micro goals and power through them, get some help, or delegate.

To create a sense of structure and accomplishment as you move through the exercises in this book, I've created the ultimate POP System Checklist. As you complete the exercises found in each chapter, flip back to this chart and mark each one as done. You may want to revisit some exercises. Moving through the process, you may find—I hope you find!—that some of your initial responses and thoughts shift and move. Give yourself permission to change your mind. Go back and make changes. But most important, acknowledge the work you're doing by undertaking this process. Engaging in self-reflection and establishing new habits and patterns is hard work and you should give yourself credit for it.

We have covered an incredible amount of information in the book and it's a lot to take in, so first, I would like to highlight the CliffsNotes version of each chapter. With each quick refresher, take the time to look at each chapter's exercises, and if you haven't done them already, now would be a good time to get them done. They will all be necessary for starting your thirty-day POP plan at the end of this chapter!

Here goes, deep breath . . .

Chapter 1: Defining POP (Personality, Opportunity, Productivity)

In this chapter you learned the idea of setting aside the endless to-do lists so you can create a streamlined, simplified priority list where the first item on the list is you.

Far from being selfish, this new approach to "me first" will help you to achieve an enduring legacy of self-honesty and courage, rather than allow you to be buffeted by the changing winds of cultural expectations.

Here I introduced the POP method to show you how to do that. *POP* stands for *personality*, *opportunity*, and *productivity*. This chapter explored what each concept means and how they work together (personality + opportunity = productivity) to focus your limited life energy toward the things that matter.

First, we have to understand ourselves and our personalities, so our first stop was creating a **POP Personality Profile**, highlighting the importance of digging into who you really are. Sometimes there are surface things we don't like, and so it takes courage and brutal honesty to write down the truths that most define us.

These are not easy questions, but once you have discovered the blueprint of who you are, you can start to make decisions that support, rather than sabotage, that blueprint. Women—both historically and today—have focused on trying to prove ourselves, by trying to get the *maximum* amount of things done in whatever time we have. We want to have spotless houses, gourmet meals, executive-track promotions, well-behaved children, a robust spiritual life, a spotless community-service record, and, on top of it all, we want time to just relax. We see ourselves as failures and as simply not good enough. So instead of spending time working on ourselves and knowing and loving who we really are, we base our value on what we've crossed off on our to-do lists. We spread ourselves thin through overcommitting, overvolunteering, and holding ourselves up to standards that are near impossible to achieve, and when we fail (because really, we were sabotaging ourselves from the start), we mentally bludgeon ourselves for not being good enough. We are mice in a wheel, "accomplishing" a lot, but we are not getting anywhere that really matters to us.

In this section, we also redefined productivity—to show you how to shift your mind-set about getting things done as well as realign your expectations about how your days should look and feel. Productivity will no longer be about getting the most done that you possibly can in the shortest amount of time. Productivity will be about stripping everything away but the core of your life purpose, and then taking action on only those goals.

Here's the Drill

- ❏ Personality questionnaire
- ❏ Personality summation

❑ Roadblocks, detours, and open roads

❑ Perfect day, real day

Chapter 2: The Only Approval You Need Is Your Own

In this chapter, we discussed the importance of being an *observer* of your own life. This is the core mind-set shift that thousands of self-empowerment articles boil down to: to change your life, you must remain present in your life. *You must hush the internal critic, stop your ears to the external pressures of society, and silence the siren call of numbing tactics* (whether it's mindless eating, drinking, Instagramming, or anything else that you may be using to escape reality). This is the first step to taking one's internal and external world into one's own hands and being present with each moment, rather than frustrated, disappointed, and divided.

For centuries, it's been near impossible for women to make choices that align with their true goals, rather than the goals that have been foisted upon them. We have been watched, judged, and examined, and as a result we have worked and behaved to please others instead of ourselves. This is why we're constantly trying to do so much—if we're not keeping everyone around us happy, we feel that we're not enough. So **in order to take control of our life, happiness, and productivity we have to no longer react to how others perceive us.** Instead, we learned how to actively create (and validate) our perception of ourselves in the world.

This chapter also discussed how to detach from others' opinions of how and why we're operating the way we are. Breaking the habit of constantly looking for approval or a reaction is difficult to do in this instant gratification society, but it's essential to help women transition from the observed to the observer.

Here's the Drill

- ☐ Name a time when you haven't acted, out of fear or concern of judgment.

- ☐ Name a time when you acted without (or in spite of) concern of judgment.

- ☐ Whose judgment do you think of most?

- ☐ Name a time when you had to be in front of people and were worried about your appearance or judgment.

- ☐ Name your three strongest qualities.

- ☐ Name your three most original qualities.

- ☐ Remind yourself of these before a challenging moment.

Chapter 3: You and Your Smart Mouth

In this chapter, we challenged the conventional idea that saying yes moves you forward and saying no keeps you standing still. We examined how the courage that it takes to say no allows you to get the things you *actually* want, rather than the things others want you to want.

This chapter also focused on the words that are most typically used to define women and to keep them down and unhappy. We evaluated how we use language that can undermine our value. In particular, women have a tendency to constantly apologize when they have nothing to apologize for. Being in perpetual apology mode undermines your message, and it projects an image that you are powerless over your actions and reactions (an image that often becomes internalized and creates a negative feedback loop). The apology mind-set must be cleared out of the way before lasting change can take root.

Women are constantly saying yes when we want (and need) to say no. Why? Because we are encouraged to be polite and being polite always seems to trump being frank and honest. **Life is not a popularity contest if you want to be happy.** I hate this notion of being polite, and I want women to see why it hurts them. Instead, we should seek to be kind, not polite. However, saying yes is much easier (and makes us more friends) than no. In this chapter, **we learned to let go of mindless yeses, the** *should*, **and the apology mind-set, and instead learned to proudly say no to what doesn't serve us.**

Here's the Drill

- ❏ Name some "yes" scenarios.

- ❏ Name things you'd like to say no to.

- ❏ Practice saying no.

- ❏ Take note of your *sorry*s in a day

- ❏ What are your *should*s? Can you lose some?

Chapter 4: How the Internet Changed the Game for Women

In this chapter, we highlighted the amazing thing about the time in which we're living: it really feels like all the **progress online has been an incredible gift for women—assuming we use it correctly**. The internet can be our best friend or our worst enemy. Now, moms can work from home. We can choose our own schedules. We can embark on a side hustle by putting energy into a hobby that could become a business. But more and more, we find ourselves using this powerful resource to compare our lives to others and berate ourselves for our less-than-picture-perfect lives. We also learned of many success stories of women who were able to build an online presence and turn it into a thriving business—opportunities that would have previously been unavailable to them.

Finally, we analyzed all the ways the internet can (a) really help us and (b) hinder us if used incorrectly.

Here's the Drill

- ❏ Name three ways you're able to use the internet to make your life run more efficiently.

- ❏ Name three times social media has made you feel worse.

- ❏ How much time daily do you *think* you spend on social networks?

- ❏ List three ways you could organize your online time to support you rather than control you.

Chapter 5: Why You Should Stop Doing Everything and Start Focusing on Just Three Areas (Seriously)

This is a big one! Here I spoke of the importance of creating a life plan for yourself by creating three big goals that you can work toward to achieve fulfillment and be truly productive. How you get to these three goals is just as important as the goals themselves. Through the process of defining the three areas of your life—aligning you with your newfound POP—you will now start to be able to trade mediocrity for happiness. When you focus on these three areas with clarity it will help define the choices you make in how you spend your time and energy. Here begins a **journey of self-discovery that will lead you to the three most important aspects of your life where you will not only be productive but also produce happiness for yourself (and those around you).**

Here's the Drill

- ❒ List your goals.

- ❒ Narrow down your goals to the Big 3 in career growth, personal growth, and relationship growth.

- ❒ Align personal statement with goals.

Chapter 6: The Importance of Outsourcing

Once you make the commitment to your Big 3 choices, you will need to let go of the activities and actions that are no longer part of them and that are holding you back.

In this section, we take a close look at how you spend your time throughout the day and the activities you engage in. **You need to ask yourself exacting questions about how (and if) each thing you do puts effort and energy toward your three choices.** This analysis is designed to make you stop, slow down, and really face the truth of what your life looks like, and why it looks that way.

When we reduce the time we spend on mundane, if necessary, tasks we are freed up to work toward our greater goals and experience moments of happiness more often and more deeply. With this freedom, women can make great strides, both from a career and a personal happiness standpoint.

Here's the Drill

☐ Seven-Day Time-Track Challenge: Note how you're spending your time, hourly or daily, for one week. Be sure to pay attention to how you're feeling and whether the way you spend time is supporting your Big 3 goals.

☐ What are the tasks that make you feel most stretched?

☐ What are the jobs you intend on outsourcing? Make a note about how you'll get these items off your list.

Chapter 7: How to Use Your Time Much Better Than You Are Right Now

Now that you understand how you can save some time by eliminating or outsourcing much of what doesn't serve you, this chapter talks about how to maximize the time you spend on the stuff that moves you closer to your Big 3. In other words, how do you actually achieve your goals? Here I introduced the concept of micro goals, which will play in tandem with your larger, macro goals that make up the Big 3. This chapter showed how to infuse little boosts of energy into your days to help you stay motivated and inspired. Additionally, it introduced the concept of productivity sprints—or high-intensity interval training for the brain. Using these sprints, you can multiply your output in 10- to 15-minute sprint sessions, thus reaching your target, and still have time left over for the things that make you happy.

Here's the Drill

- ❏ Make a list of the three tasks you most look forward to. These are your flow tasks.

- ❏ Make a list of the three tasks you wish you could avoid. These are your sprint tasks.

- ❏ List three to five nonwork items you're going to add to your weekly schedule that will improve your life balance (e.g., sex, a walk, reading, a bath, brunch with friends).

- ❏ Create an ideal daily schedule in which each day includes an aspect of each of your Big 3 goals.

Chapter 8: Assemble Your POP Posse

This was a big chapter as well, as it focused on a potentially touchy subject. Throughout this book, we've held up to the light and examined the poorly thought-out choices we make when our only goal is to get as much done as possible. In this chapter, we did the same for the personal influences in our lives, examining them one by one, and either polishing them or discarding them. The truth is, some people drain you. Some people lift you up. Some people take. Some people give. In order to have the most productive ecosystem around you, **you have to analyze the people you spend the most time with and critically evaluate whether they're a destructive or constructive force.** Those relationships that aren't productive need to go (or at least be pushed to the back burner), and those that help you thrive should be put front and center. Again, life isn't a popularity contest—**it's about feeling loved and valued by the right people, not by all people.**

Here's the Drill

- ❏ List the people you spend time with daily.

- ❏ Note how you feel when you're with them.

- ❏ Note the values you share with them.

- ❏ Who do you share good news with?

- ❏ Who do you not share good news with?

- ❏ What do you want to learn from a mentor?

PHEW.

Now that you've done all that, it's time to actually start moving toward your success story. And the good news is that the formula is easy. You've already done the hard part. To create your thirty-day POP plan we will simply do a week-by-week charting of how you will spend your time, making sure to include all your goals.

Start by mapping out week ONE:

On either a large calendar or a digital calendar, or in a journal, write down your seven-day, Monday-to-Sunday schedule. Include everything from the time you wake up to all your meetings and encounters throughout the day, to your evening and sleep plan. Use five different-colored markers (or fonts) to denote which tasks represent your Big 3, a fourth for miscellaneous, and a fifth to represent things that you actually feel are killing/wasted time. If there are any potentially challenging parts to your week, make sure to schedule five minutes in advance of each to find stillness and calm in your mind, reminding yourself of your strengths to conscientiously channel success.

At the end of each day, make notes on how you felt throughout the day — what gave you energy and what depleted your energy.

On Sunday (or your seventh day), schedule out forty-five minutes to review all your notes. Jot down which activities most brought you closer to your Big 3 and which set you back. Using these findings, fill in your schedule for the new week starting the following day.

Repeat for the entire month.

At the end of month one, you will start to see that by diligently tracking your moves, analyzing how they either bring you closer to or further from your goals, and then pivoting accordingly you will start to have real momentum.

If you repeat this method for the next two months you should get to a point where you are fully in a groove with yourself and more and more will no longer need to rely on rigorous scheduling. At the end of three months, you should be able to now make moves based on a proven intuition and a solidly built set of habits. This is where you want to be. Moving in a free-flowing state, by listening to yourself and truly knowing where you are and where you need to be.

Finally, once you've reached this state of automatic pilot, it is still imperative that you check in with yourself—take maybe forty-five minutes—to make sure your Big 3 are still fresh in your mind and that they still reflect the goals you want to achieve most. It may also be helpful monthly, or anytime you are feeling "off-course," to refer back to this chapter for a quick refresher.

CHAPTER TEN

Avoiding Burnout

France, August 2011: *En vacances! (On vacation!)*

As our aircraft began its descent, I hurriedly went over all the work that I had prepared and prescheduled to go out on social over my ten-day vacation in France—*my first real vacation in two years*. At the time, I was still working at the fashion start-up, *Pick the Brain* had fully hit its stride and was taking off like wildfire, and Geri and I were in full fund-raising mode for LEAF. It wasn't the greatest time to be leaving, but then again, I'd been saying that for two years. I had emailed everyone I needed to email. I had proudly set up my OOO auto-email response to let anyone who reached out know that I was *on vacation*. Full stop.

Why then, Louis wondered aloud as we finished up packing—*seemingly irritated*—was I bringing my laptop at all, if I had no intention of working?

"I just have some last-minute things to finish up on the flight and then I'm done. Promise!" I tried to reassure him.

All he responded with was a very knowing look.

Now in the cab, whizzing from the airport to his parents' flat in Paris, I excitedly took in the city and waited for vacation mode to fully sink in. As I looked around, I noticed that many, like 90 percent, of the stores and restaurants we were passing were closed.

"It's August," Louis reminded me. "*Everything is closed*. It's summer vacation." I knew, of course, that the French (and Europeans in general) were serious about their *vacances*, but I'd forgotten they took it *this* literally. Though I was slightly bummed about the shops being closed, I quickly got over it when I reminded myself I too was on vacation, no agendas, nothing to do, *just relaxation*.

After a quick pit stop at the flat, where we showered and changed, we jumped in the car and headed straight to Normandy to visit with his parents, sisters, and cousins at the country house. It felt like we'd been on a bit of a whirlwind tour already for the past twenty-four hours, with all the trains, planes, and automobiles, but I'd rest when we got to the countryside. The next couple of days were a lot of fun, but not exactly what I would call "resting," what with seven rambunctious children all under the age of twelve wildly running around trying to get the attention of their "*oncle* Louis," conversations that required 100 percent of my concentration as I tried to navigate what was going on via my rusty French, and my brutal jet lag. I was in high spirits, but actually quite exhausted. The only saving grace was that not being able to sleep actually allowed me the opportunity to check emails late at night. And respond to a couple. I mean, I was up anyway, with Louis snoring softly-ish beside me. It just made sense, *non*?

What I hadn't factored into my in-advance work prep was the amount of real-time commenting and inquiries that came from my various social networks for *Pick the Brain*. For every article I had prescheduled on Facebook, there were dozens of comments and DMs. I was posting three times a day—so three days out of the game and I started to notice a rapid accumulation of unanswered questions and queries. They didn't take much time to respond to, but having that direct line of communication to me was crucial to my audience. I made a deal with myself that I would check in once daily, just to quickly respond to anything that seemed time-sensitive.

As we set off in the car on day four, headed southwest to Cap Ferret, I settled into vacation mode for the first time. Nine hours and some serious traffic later, we arrived at the beautiful beach house of Louis's family's friends. I was a little more tired than I had hoped, but *now* vacation would officially start.

We threw off our clothes, slid into our bathing suits, and headed down to the beach for a dip. It was perfect. As we were showering and changing before we headed down for drinks and dinner, I thought it would be a great chance to just *check in*.

Big. Mistake.

Not only did I have an email from one of my developers letting me know of an imminently pending Google algorithm change that could totally screw *Pick the Brain*—and demanding to talk strategy *immediately*—but I also had an email from one of my reports at the start-up telling me she'd heard that one of my most important employees was on the verge of quitting. I started to panic, and with the time difference, I couldn't make contact for the next couple of hours. I sent off emails to both telling them to make contact when they were at their respective offices so that we could chat. I descended to dinner . . . *with my phone*.

So while everyone else was basking in the sun by the pool, noshing on incredible cheeses and fresh bread washed down with cool, crisp glasses of rosé, I was politely dismissing myself every twenty minutes to "go to the bathroom" (check my phone). By the end of the night, (a) surely everybody must have thought I had a raging bladder infection and (b) I had made contact and communicated with both parties, but no answers were in sight.

As I crawled into bed that night, Louis asked me what was going on. I told him everything and he deeply sympathized, as he knew how important both were to me, but he was still baffled.

"But don't you have someone who can handle this for you? You're *on vacation.*"

I didn't feel like launching into my "*Bébé*, you know the internet doesn't sleep" speech that he had heard a thousand times, so I assured him all would be right by the morning and tried to sleep. I, of course, couldn't sleep between my never-ending jet lag and mounting anxiety, so I started several Gchats with people in both offices to try to solve these escalating problems.

The following morning, now extremely exhausted, I awoke to a new situation. Geri and I were deep in fund-raising mode and she'd been introduced to an investor who would be an amazing fit for us. The only problem: we needed to tweak our deck and pitch for a meeting that would be happening the day I got back. This was very exciting news. And also terrible. I would have to find the time.

Over the next few days, I spent most of my time running up and down the two hundred steps from the beach (where there was no Wi-Fi) to the house (where there was spotty Wi-Fi). Every time I would reappear, the group of cool French friends and family we were hanging with would make a shocked comment about how much I was working . . . *on vacation.* They could not wrap their heads around it—they thought it was totally insane. Many a time I overheard Louis telling them in French, "You know it's different in America . . . and the internet never sleeps . . ." I prayed it didn't sound as foolish as when I said it in English to him.

By day seven, I wasn't even pretending to take bathroom breaks or make excuses. After an hour on the beach (when my office was still closed), I would just head up to start working. Yes, now as I was waiting for responses in between emails, I was also responding to comments on social media, checking how my own personal pictures were performing on Instagram, and working on a refreshed deck. I was in a very pretty office, but an office nonetheless. I distinctly remember at one point holding my phone over my head at an oyster farm we had all waded out to, to bring back fresh oysters to eat. Luckily, my French hosts found my behavior not rude, but rather entertaining—they would poke one another and point at me like they'd just discovered a strange circus animal that had escaped, every time I tried to find a signal. Add in the fact that I'd barely found any time to tan my super fair complexion, and I was ripe for fodder at the hands of these tanned, chilled-out Mediterranean gods and goddesses.

Day eight, and things reached a climax. I had seemed to reach an agreement with my valued employee who was thinking of leaving. Geri and I were set on the deck. And the only outstanding problem was this pending Google algorithm change. This was a big deal—they had done this before, and I had seen other sites ten times the size of my blog collapse almost overnight. I had been spared in the past, but who knew what crazy things they were about to change now. (It was at this very moment that I decided I needed to change my strategy on *PTB* to be less reliant on search traffic—but that's beside the point.) My freelance developer had wanted to jump on a Skype call to finalize the changes to be made, and with the time difference it had been difficult. Trying to communicate these changes via email had also proven ineffective. The only time we could find was in the late morning of day eight, which coincided with a planned boating expedition to cross the bay and have a picnic lunch at the epic sand dunes.

I promised Louis I would be done by noon and then I would be all his.

"For the next forty-eight hours?" he said, taking a jab.

I ignored it and said I would meet everybody at the dock.

Of course, there were problems logging onto Skype and the connection was so slow that we had to keep starting and stopping. By the time we wrapped up and had a plan in place that felt good, it was twelve ten. I slammed my computer shut, grabbed my bag, and started running.

As I was about three minutes away, still at an incline on the side of the hill, I could see everyone on the dock, untying the boat. I flailed my arms in the air and called everyone's name.

"Attendez! Attendez! J'arrive!" I yelled. (Wait! Wait ! I'm coming!)

But as I finally made it onto the dock, the boat was already vanishing into the distance. I was too late. I collapsed onto the dock, my legs dangling in the water, and frantically tried to call Louis's cell. Of course, he didn't have it with him. *Why would he?* HE WAS ON VACATION.

My head in my hands, I sobbed. I felt terrible for having kept everyone waiting. People who were trying their best to entertain the un-entertainable. Not only was I late, they were going to think I hadn't even *tried* to make it. I had an awful feeling in the pit of my stomach. On top of that, I could only imagine the frustrating situation I had put Louis in.

Walking back to the house, crying, I also realized how absolutely exhausted I was. More tired than when I'd left LAX. How that was possible, I didn't know. It was like some robot had taken all control of me and I didn't know how to stop it. Everything just seemed like such an immediate problem that needed solving. And apparently I thought I was the only one who could solve everything.

As I sat by the pool, trying to drown my sorrows in a glass of perfect French wine, Louis's godmother (whose house we were staying in) descended. She was an incredible German/French beauty who had had wild success in business, and yet she was entirely effortless. It was like she floated. As she sat down beside me, I apologized profusely for my behavior over the past couple of days. She graciously said there was nothing to forgive. "Don't worry, *chérie*, it doesn't affect me at all. It's your problem, not mine."

As I was thanking her, I started to analyze her statement. *What was my problem?* So I asked her.

"You have forgotten how to relax. How to really relax. In fact, you are fighting it. You are finding every excuse in the book to distract you so you don't have to be alone with yourself and relax. And what's *zee* point? After all, success means nothing if you can't really enjoy it."

I stared at her, wide-eyed, eating up everything she had to say.

"But you won't have to worry about that much longer, because at this rate you won't be that successful. You will have burned out long before you've gotten to where you want to go . . ."

And with that, she stood and grabbed the ice bucket on her way out.

"More wine?" Her question hung in the air. And just like that, not waiting for a response, she was gone.

POP *Truth:*

YOU'RE SUPPOSED TO ENJOY THE RIDE.

✦ Success at any cost?

✦ Invest in your own well-being.

The moral of the story may seem obvious. It certainly did to me as I wrote it. What is so scary, though, is how far removed I was from what was actually happening in the moment. That hamster wheel is very hypnotic. The great thing I took away from this experience is that the more I am doing just to get things done, to feel busy, important, or needed, the further I get from who I am. The more distractions I put into place just so I don't have to sit with myself, the further I get from what I really want, from what should bring me energy instead of deplete me.

At the end of the day, this is not a sustainable model—mental and quite probably physical burnout are assured. But even if it were tenable to continue this way, where would it lead? Nowhere. At least, nowhere you would want to be, if you really asked yourself the question. We have worked very hard to get to this place in our lives and in history, it would be such a shame to, rather than hit full stride, run like frantic maniacs throughout the most vibrant part of our lives, only to fizzle out just before we've truly made it.

In the story I shared, there is no question that 80 percent of the stuff I *needed to get to* could have been handled by others, 10 percent didn't need to be handled at all in that brief window, and the remaining 10 percent (the pitch deck with Geri) could have been managed differently. What's more, I could have been far more effective, both personally and for my businesses, returning from vacation well-rested and reenergized, rather than just as tired as when I left but with better Instagram pics.

When the creative director Linda Honan left Australia for New York, she was full of energy and enthusiasm for the adventures she felt sure were ahead of her. And sure enough, all the work and passion she poured into her career paid off. A decade of nonstop work resulted in promotion after promotion. "It was exciting but also a physically gruelling life to live, because I was burning the candle at both ends. My foot was on the accelerator for a good decade."

As satisfying as this time was, toward the end of it, Linda started to notice her once-boundless energy and passion starting to fade. "There was not the pep in my step that I was used to feeling, and I started to question whether I was really doing the things I was best at." Part of the problem was that she'd had so many promotions that she was no longer as hands-on with the projects she was overseeing. That creative work that she'd always loved seemed at a distance. Also, as she climbed the corporate ladder of agency life, the work became, well, more corporate. She just wasn't feeling as connected to the work. Would a new job at a different firm revive her? Or would it be more of the same? She felt lost.

"I felt like I'd lost my shimmer and I didn't know how to get it back, and that was very scary for me. I remember having dinner with a wonderful friend who is a very strong female entrepreneur, and she said to me, 'I think you are trying to be like a monkey: you won't let go of one branch, your fists are so tightly gripped on this one branch and you won't let go of it until you've got a new plan. But you're so tired that you might not be able to come up with the answer for what's next. So why don't you free-fall? Why don't you just drop? What if you didn't have a plan and decided to do something different even though you don't know what that is?' And I said to her that night, 'That's ridiculous, I couldn't do that, what would I tell everyone? I'm the girl who always has a plan.' So then I went home and I went to bed. Then I woke up the next morning and I opened my eyes and said, 'I'm actually going to do that.' "

And she did. She rented out her apartment, left behind concerns about what other people would think, and headed off to visit a friend in South America. She traveled around Brazil, went to the Amazon, climbed the Andes. Although Linda had always traveled a lot, this was the first time she'd actually disconnected from work, from the millions of emails, from needing to be one call away from a project. Those six months of just traveling gave her the break she needed to think about what she really wanted. While hiking up the Andes, she unpacked her experiences in New York—what had been energizing, what had been depleting—and came to the realization that she felt most excited when she worked with other creators. "I felt like entrepreneurs were my Holy Grail and I was excited being close to that and seeing their vision."

At the end of that time, a great job opportunity came up in London. "But listening to my intuition, I couldn't get back into that world." And that new practice of slowing down, of listening to her own intuition, has changed how she approaches work now. Based in L.A., Linda now only works on projects she feels a personal connection to, with people she feels like she's got something to learn from or whose values she admires or feels an alignment with. She's found herself drawn to working with female entrepreneurs. Her work ethic is as evident as ever, but now her work is fueled by a real excitement in the work she's doing.

Now that you have a system in place for reaching your goals while maintaining balance in your life, you have to be careful to not drive back into the burnout lane.

EXHAUSTION VERSUS BURNOUT

What exactly is burnout anyway? Is it simply being tired? Not really. Lots of things make us tired but not burnt-out. A day that is full with work, a run through the park, then time spent with friends can have you collapsing into your bed in a heap, but not leave you feeling that emptied-out depletion associated with burnout. If it's just fatigue that's slowing you down, then getting to bed a bit earlier for a night or two will sort you out. Burnout is not that. Think of it as tired plus. The American Psychiatric Association defines burnout with three factors.

1. **Emotional exhaustion.** Fatigue is part of burnout, and feeling tired even when you're not at work, but this chronic state means you're feeling low in energy consistently.

2. **Lost sense of self.** When you find yourself having negative thoughts about yourself and others, being quicker than normal to criticize, and struggle to find empathy.

3. **Sense of failure.** You're doubting yourself and your abilities and feeling underappreciated.

In other words, burnout is a mental and emotional state, more than simply a physical one. The APA also points out that while burnout is not the same as depression, its existence can be a sign that you're on the path to depression. In other words, this is serious. Many women tolerate a burnout state as if it's just part of the gig of being a busy, capable person, when in fact, burnout will diminish your ability to function at a high level. Women, in particular, are susceptible to burnout given the expectations that we will not only kick ass at work all day, but then go home and look after both chores and everyone's happiness there.

It is crucial that we apply these thoughts on burnout not solely to our workplace behavior, but to our home life as well. You home is a place where you should find happiness and calm. A place to restore yourself. It is not a place for you to walk through the door and then start on another to-do list, *home version*. Sure, there is a lot of stuff that needs to get done—but there's also a lot of stuff that doesn't need to get done, and most certainly not by you. I understand that most of us want to be perfect in every way (or feel bad that we don't) but nobody is really appreciating all of this overachiever home effort. There is simply, as with everything, a point of diminishing returns. You must identify this point so you don't start suffering burnout from your home. To avoid this very serious type of burnout, you need to start viewing your home as a protected space, not as a place where a lot of *stuff* gets done. Because you're trading the really good stuff—calm, serenity, love, focus, relationships—for disposable stuff. Flashing back to my French vacation example, the same ideals can be applied. You don't need to do everything. Give up the control and allow those you love to help. Empower them. It will energize you.

Knowing that the world is set up to steer you toward burnout, you have to be conscious in your choices in order to avoid it. But avoid it you can, by paying attention to some nonnegotiables.

HOW NOT TO BURN OUT: LIVE IN YOUR VALUES

The fastest route to burnout is to spend time on things you don't believe in. In fact, you could have the breeziest schedule, but if it only contained work or tasks you weren't connected to, you'd quickly begin to feel depleted. Likewise, you can push yourself quite hard if your time is spent on activities that fill you with satisfaction. You're probably going to be just fine.

To know the difference between those two very different kinds of busy is about knowing yourself. When I spoke to the psychiatrist Dr. Anita Chakrabarti about this, it was something she was very familiar with in her practice. If you're feeling drained by your life, the first step in fixing it may involve a mirror. "Taking time to reflect on what you value is really important, and are your actions actually mirroring your values? I think a lot of people in their thirties and forties find that they're running in this machine that does not necessarily reflect their values." This spillover into your thirties and forties comes from not having taken the time to start discovering who you really are and outlining a plan for yourself (something we've spent much time talking about) in your twenties. You have to take the time to consider what you value and whether your time and energy are moving toward or away from those values. "If your behavior and your values don't match, that's when you start to feel like you're having a breakdown. If your behavior and values match up, you can tolerate or bear a lot.

If you're doing actions that you don't even value, then you start to feel really overwhelmed."

OHM EVERY DAY

Knowing who you are and what you care about is a habit like any other. Put everyone else first, notice how they're feeling, be sensitive to their needs often enough, and you'll be really good at it. Oh, right, you're already doing that. If you want to stay in balance by knowing your own thoughts and needs, you'll have to put some time toward that also. Spending a small amount of time daily in meditation will give you the skills you need to check in with yourself. Quieting your busy, workday brain and breathing for just five or ten minutes allows a deeper self-knowledge to develop. It's harder to make the choices that lead to burnout when you're consistently checking in with yourself.

Pro tip: My two favorite apps for beginner meditation are:

1 Giant Mind: In my opinion, this is the simplest way to dive in. Starts with a great twelve-day program to ease you into being alone with yourself and then takes you into a full experience with various options.

Headspace: With many more bells and whistles, such as time tracking and a social option to "buddy up" with friends, it has all the classic elements of how to meditate but many more features.

Finally, my favorite breathing exercise is one I use before I meditate and before I go to sleep each night. Dr. Andrew Weil's 4-7-8 breathing technique has been an amazing aid to get me settled quickly, and it's super easy.

Sit comfortably. Close your eyes. Place the tip of your tongue up against the back of your top front teeth. Breathe in through your nose for four consistent beats. Hold your breath for seven consistent beats. Breathe out through your mouth, with some force, for eight consistent beats. Repeat four times.

Though it may seem simple, I swear by it—once you've formed the habit it has an immediate calming effect. For more detail, search "Dr. Andrew Weil 4-7-8 Breathing" on YouTube.

CREATE BOUNDARIES

Earlier in the book we talked about adding *no* to your vocabulary and what a scary step that is to take. That fear is legitimate. If you say no to answering emails that come into your inbox at 8:30 p.m., will your boss take note of it? If you say no to meetings that are making your schedule look like a patchwork quilt (and productive work next to impossible), will your next performance review take a nosedive? If you say no to volunteering at your kid's school, will the other moms judge you?

There's no doubt that setting boundaries comes with an element of risk. You can't always know how people around you will react to a new approach from you. If you're someone who has always said yes to everything and you suddenly change your tune, people may not like it. Change can be hard. On the other hand, we know the result of saying yes to every damn thing—hi, burnout!—and you're committing to avoiding that narrative. The bottom line is, if you want people to start treating you in a different way, you're going to have to train them—starting with yourself.

First, you need to decide which boundaries will be most meaningful to you. Think about the demands in your life that leave you feeling pulled thin. Are you not giving yourself enough restorative time away from work? Did you overcommit to a volunteer project that you immediately regretted? Does your family believe you're the only person who can operate the washing machine? Start with one and come up with a plan to get this obligation off your plate by communicating that you won't be doing it anymore. Now, I'm not suggesting that you have a diva moment and throw your responsibilities to the wind. Help smooth things over by offering an alternate arrangement. At first, this is going to feel like another item on your to-do list. So much so that you may feel like it's not worth it. Do not give in to this impulse! Invest some time into getting back some time for yourself.

If your manager at work is in the habit of firing off emails throughout the evening, it can feel like you have no choice but to reply immediately. In a competitive environment where everyone is on call all the time, it's a legit source of stress. But if productivity is what your boss is after, it's worth it to have an explicit conversation with him or her, explaining that you'd like to improve your performance by protecting your downtime. There's more than enough evidence to back up this statement and many companies (and countries!) have policies for protecting employees' rights to nonwork hours.

When the task you need off your plate is domestic, you can follow a similar path. Let your family know that there's going to be a redistribution of chores. Explain your reasons: you want to be less stressed and happier at home, and sharing more of the chores at home would really help you with that. Come prepared with some suggestions. A ten-year-old can be taught how to handle a load or two of laundry per week, an eight-year-old can take the garbage to the chute, your mate can start handling breakfast-making duty. Let them know that at first, you'll be reminding them about their new chore, but that ultimately you'd like it to be handled without a reminder. And then—and this is big—you have to allow for these chores to happen in a way that's different from how you'd do it. If that breakfast is a bowl of cereal when you used to make overnight chia puddings? Big deal. The quickest way to suppress these efforts is to critique them.

BE IN CHARGE OF YOUR TIME

One of the reasons most people burn out is that they allow their schedules to rule them. The calendar is their master, and if a lot needs to get done, then more and more of that calendar gets blacked out. More meetings, more deadlines, more obligations. A calendar week that has no time for socializing, exercise, or family is a problem. A schedule that doesn't allow time for you to even stop and eat a meal (desk meals don't count!) is a problem. Once in a while there may be an exceptional deadline that means important energy-giving activities have to fall away. But if it's not once in a while, if it's the norm, you know you're on your way to burnout. Commit to the activities you know make you a whole person, and balance your obligation calendar with these items.

Also, and maybe even more important, be aware that many times people will fill up their calendars so they don't have to think, so they don't have to be alone with themselves. The busier you are, and especially over time, the further you get away from who you really are and where you really should be. Understanding this is crucial to optimal, *real* efficiency.

Lori Deschene, the creator of the wildly popular health and wellness site *Tiny Buddha*, told me about her own relationship with her calendar. As a freelancer at the beginning of her career, she would jump at any opportunity to write. She's learned from experience that when she's frustrated with herself, it's a sign that she's taken on too much and is flirting with burnout. "I remember at one point, I was looking at all the things I didn't finish on my to-do list and I thought, *Okay, I have worked twelve hours today. What more could I have done?* Then I realized the problem isn't me, it's my to-do list. I did not do only as much as I could have, but more. I worked literally every waking hour and at peak capacity for most of it. That's when I realized that the dissatisfaction with myself is usually a sign that I was trying to do too much. Because I know that I'm someone who does good work. I'm not someone who goes half in. I do give it my all. So if I still wasn't happy with myself, then there's probably too much on my plate."

SLEEP

I know, I just told you that burnout is not the same as being tired. However, consistently not caring for yourself in basic ways, like getting proper sleep and eating healthy foods, are great ways to push you toward a decline in energy and, eventually, burnout. The most radical act of adult self-care is to set yourself a bedtime. When there's too much on your to-do list, it can feel like the only way to make your way through it is to stay up later. But lack of sleep is pretty much at the top of the list of health, creativity, and happiness killers. Every part of our being—our bodies, our minds, our emotions—requires the intricate reboot that occurs while we sleep. People who often lack sleep, like insomniacs, almost always have other chronic health issues, such as high blood pressure, heart disease, anxiety, and depression, to name just a few.

We need seven to nine hours of sleep per night, according to the National Sleep Foundation. Yet 40 percent of Americans get six or less hours of sleep per night.

In order to achieve the baseline number of hours you need, you need to make sleep a priority. Here's a line from the National Sleep Foundation that struck me as obvious, but also profound: "Don't make it the thing you do only after everything else is done—stop doing other things so you get the sleep you need." If you struggle with making this happen, set an alarm on your phone to remind you that it's time to start winding down.

We discussed in earlier chapters the importance of morning rituals, and the end of the day also benefits hugely from the addition of ritual. Turn off electronics, spend some time with a book, meditate to clear your mind, have sex. You can decide for yourself how the end of your day should look. There are many ways to ease yourself out of your day and into sleep, and the more consistent you are about these rituals, the quicker your body and mind will be to respond to them. Just like building your muscles at the gym, with consistency and repetition, the "sleep" muscle should have *at least* as much attention paid to it, as it's the rebirth or resetting of your system, daily.

Pro tip: Just like everything else we've talked about, sleeping requires a little self-evaluation. For most of my life I have been a terrible sleeper, and it wasn't until I made it a real priority to get to the root of the problem that I got any relief. A big part of that relief came from a critical analysis of how I was (or wasn't) sleeping. Enter:

> **The Sleep Cycle alarm clock:** This app allows you to analyze your quality of sleep, how much sleep you are getting, and if you are snoring and interrupting your sleep—and the information you get is really valuable. You can start personally charting which nights you got a good sleep and what you did differently from those you didn't get a good sleep. As well, the alarm wakes you up, slowly, in your lightest sleep phase so your transition to consciousness is less jarring and you awake feeling more refreshed. I highly recommend anyone with even minor sleep problems to give it a try, as it has totally changed my life.

Understanding and navigating burnout is the last step in creating a life plan for yourself that includes success, happiness, fulfillment, and a true sense that you have been productive in your life. By managing your physical and emotional states once you've got your processes in place and being able to consistently take a "self-temperature" reading will ensure that all the hard work you've put in on the front end continues well into your future and beyond. And just remember, there will always be something else you feel you need to get done, but how many times will you have the chance to sip a great rosé on a beach in the south of France? Make everything count, so you can make it last.

EPILOGUE

Now What?

*O*ver the course of the past sixty thousand words or so, I have shared many stories in order to highlight the extreme learning (and self-reflection) curve I took to eventually discover some pretty fundamental truths about the way I was living my life, treating my relationships, and handling my business. It has been a long road, but an ultimately very fulfilling one, because I learned two major things: the power of the opportunity that we, as women, have right now, and the necessity for creating a personalized definition of productivity if we are to seize this opportunity. It's crucial that we find balance, fulfillment, and energy from within ourselves, our relationships, and our careers on our own terms.

So just when you think you've got it figured out, you get thrown a curve ball—that's the beauty of life. After all, if everything were perfect all the time, we'd be seriously fucking bored.

At the beginning of this book, I cited one of my favorite quotes in referring to a journey I started nearly twenty years ago, but it bears repeating:

"If you want to make God laugh, tell Him your plans."

And just as I'm about to wrap up my first book, highlighting parts of this long, multichaptered journey, I am reminded once again of just how true this quote is.

Two months before the first draft of this book was due, Geri and I were enthusiastically working on the latest iteration of LEAF—a subscription service called The Year of Wellness, where members would receive a monthly box themed all around one of the major principles of wellness (think detox, rest, glow, etc.). We had been given a six-month trial period to get people signed up and excited. Immediately after launch, the buzz was off the charts. We had been written up in *Self*, *InStyle*, *Forbes*, *WWD*, *mindbodygreen*, *Well+Good*, *LA Confidential*, and the list went on and on. Between the great press and our small test group, Geri and I were excited for the first time in a while about where LEAF could go. Besides that, the deep dive into the world of wellness was really up our alley. After six years of creating thousands of videos, developing an amazing audience of women, and cultivating many incredible brand relationships, we truly believed we were onto the next big thing for LEAF.

It felt good.

Tasked with mapping out how we would bring this test concept to mass scale, we worked diligently on creating a plan. We tapped some of the biggest creatives, branding experts, and lifestyle influencers to be a part of The Year of Wellness 2.0. There was a real excitement from anybody and everybody to be a part of this new vision.

When we pitched the program to our new boss (we never quite got used to this idea), there was a muted excitement. He wondered how it would be possible to launch this new arm of the business while still running our vigorous content production. After much deliberation, Geri and I agreed we would have to compromise on the content— which had been our bread and butter for the past six years—to go for the gold, which we believed lay in these boxes. It was a huge decision, full of risk, and therefore very scary, but we were united in our vision that it was not only the right move but the only one. Our one condition was that we would have to do it the right way—with no costs cut—if it were to be the success we thought it could be.

After back-and-forth meetings with our new boss, who handled all things ecommerce, we felt like we were really getting somewhere. Until we weren't.

I walked into my office, much like I did every Monday morning: mildly anxious to see what the week would bring, but excited about our new direction and happy to catch up with the team.

Ten minutes later, Geri joined me and we set about scheduling the rest of our day—we were in the final stages of our new venture, waiting for sign-off from the powers that be.

Then something strange happened. At the same moment, we both received meeting invites, fifteen minutes apart, from the head of human resources and our boss. What was even more strange was that Geri and I wouldn't be together in the meeting. *We were never separated.* (In fact, we were together so much that our nickname was Gerin.)

What could this be about? we whispered to one another. Theories began to fly. But nothing we came up with made sense.

I was first up. I walked to the conference room where the meeting was to take place.

My legs felt like concrete.

As I swung open the glass door, both my boss and the head of HR were waiting for me. They both held file folders in their hands. Neither met my gaze.

Less than seven minutes later I swung open the same glass door and walked out of the conference room, with phrases like *"it's a business decision . . ."; "we've got so much respect . . ."; "what you've built is incredible . . ."* swishing around in my head.

The details are irrelevant, but the long and short are not. We had taken a firm position in what we thought was necessary to take the business to the next level. They disagreed. We wouldn't compromise. Neither would they.

In less than seven minutes, everything we had worked for over the past six-plus years was suddenly, *shockingly*, over.

Back in my office, I rapidly fired off the highlight reel to Geri before her meeting. She stood looking back at me, speechless. Then she, too, was off.

As I fell back into my chair, waiting for her to return, I contemplated what had just transpired. I was truly shocked. This hadn't been part of the plan.

It wasn't good. It wasn't bad. It was . . . *nothing*.

When Geri returned, with the same news, she, too, plopped down in her chair.

We looked at each other and then, after a long pause, started to laugh. And once we started, we couldn't stop. I'm not sure if it was nervous energy or just really necessary relief, but I hadn't laughed that hard in a long time.

Once we calmed down, I asked, "How do you feel?"

She paused, then looked up at me and said, "Honestly, *relieved*."

And in perhaps the most shocking turn of the day, I said, "I couldn't agree more."

In truth, not twenty-four hours prior, I had stood in my living room, nervously recounting to Louis how much work I still had left to do on the book. I had no clue how I was going to be able to get it done. And now, here I sat, with apparently all the time in the world.

Because of the deal we had struck when we sold the business, we had big severance packages and were offered health insurance until the end of our contracts, so financially we were basically in the same position as if we'd been working until the end of the year. This greatly helped soften our rapid departure.

What makes this story all the more complex, however, is the second twist of fate. Just one month prior to our big split, I had discovered, quite surprisingly, that I was pregnant. After years of trying, and almost giving up, I sat staring at two blue lines on a pregnancy test in disbelief. It was so early on, and knowing that anything could happen, I'd told almost nobody. I had only told Geri the week prior. So to now suddenly find myself pregnant and out of my main squeeze for a job was going to take a second to get used to.

By all accounts, the old Erin would have probably freaked out and made rash decisions. After all, I now had to deliver a book, then deliver a baby, with no certainty about anything past that. Add raging hormones into the mix and there was definitely the potential for a meltdown. So I waited for the anxiety to strike. For the uncertainty to sink in and start taking its toll. But two months later, nothing. And I'm no longer waiting. I am filled with a sense of peace and calm, excited not anxious.

What's the difference this time around?

I have a process in place.

I know who I am. And I am confident in that.

I know what I want. And I am confident in that.

I now have a deep awareness about all facets of my life—a study and practice that continues daily.

I understand, on a profound level, what it is like to waste time and energy. *A lot of time and energy.* And I've learned the incalculable value of protecting these things.

Because I've found balance through my processes, choosing what matters most across all aspects of my life, I don't feel the need to run to find "an answer" to my new realities. I have done the work and I trust, completely, the process. I understand the answer will come to me if I continue to do the work in a mindful way and am receptive to what the universe suggests.

Finally, I understand the power and the opportunity of the times we are living in *now*. Not only do I believe that I am uniquely positioned to be the most productive, fulfilled version of myself because of all the work that I have done, but I believe that WE, as women, are uniquely positioned, in the wake of the digital era, to step up and take what is rightfully ours. There is a sense of camaraderie, understanding, and excitement among us—either conscious or subconscious—*that we're onto something*. We're pounding at that glass ceiling. We're protesting together. We're standing up for one another. We are embracing all the powers of femininity while discarding antiquated notions of being ladylike. And unlike at any other time in history, we have the tools of the internet at our disposal and ready to help. All we've got to do is learn to use them in the right way. Whether you are in the internet business, a doctor, a waitress, a stay-at-home mom, the tools are there to reorganize the way you are working, living, and *thinking*. It's taken us two thousand–plus years to get here. Let's not fuck it up. Or let anybody else fuck it up for us.

Life is undoubtedly complex. Necessarily complex. But how you approach it should be simple. That doesn't mean it won't take a lot of work. Simplicity is often the hardest thing to achieve. But in simplicity—by stripping your goals back to three things that help you move forward in a productive way, saying what you mean, knowing clearly who you are, accepting nothing less than you deserve, creating a crystal-clear plan for yourself—you will find beauty, energy, and strength. These are things that will truly allow you to live a productive life.

So what's next for me? I'm not sure. What I do know, however, is that even though there is uncertainty, I'm not uncertain. I am no longer scared by, but rather am excited by, what's to come.

That's the power of knowing how to #GetShitDone.

So what are you waiting for?

Acknowledgments

At the beginning of this book I referenced how, early on, I expected to be giving a thank-you speech at the Academy Awards, right after George Clooney handed me my Oscar and his number. But as I sit here today, I can't think of anything better than being able to publicly thank everyone who helped me along the way to write this book.

Now the only thing I still long for is *Amal's* number.

I could not have done anything close to what I have achieved without the love and unconditional support of my family. A heartfelt thanks to my dad, Clark, who is himself a writer and my constant inspiration. Thanks to my mom, Johan, a fantastic example of a strong woman who knows how to get things done. And to my brother, Harris, for being my lifelong sidekick. A huge thanks to my stepmom, Anita, who was probably my biggest supporter to keep working on this book—and who helped out so much with the actual process. And finally, to my stepdad, Rod, whose positivity and enthusiasm know no bounds!

Many thanks to my #girlboss of an agent, Maria Ribas, at Stonesong, who had championed me and the idea for this book long before it ever started to take shape. To my editor, Diana Ventimiglia, and my publisher, Michele Martin, at North Star Way/Simon & Schuster, for taking a huge chance on an unknown writer. Your gusto for this project was a huge motivating factor, and I literally couldn't have done this without you.

Thank you so much to the strong women who lent their voices and expertise to this project: Jaclyn Johnson, Linda Honan, Alexia Brue, Sam Negrin, Jane Francisco, Jewel Burks, Lori Deschene, Tracy Moore, Leah Mclaren, and Ceri Marsh. Thank you for not only providing great insight into this project, but for all the inspiration you give to young women on a daily basis.

A very special thanks to my partner in crime at LEAF, and contributor to this book, Geri Hirsch—whom I have learned so much from and with.

For their general support and real-life inspiration, thanks to my best pals Kayleen, Sophie, Larissa, Shereen, Peggy, and Melu.

And last but not least, *mille bisous à mon partenaire, Louis, qui n'a de patience et d'amour que de me donner. Merci! Merci!*

And now as the orchestra begins to play and the teleprompter reads "Wrap it up . . ."

One last thanks, to the Santa Monica Public Library, for letting me use their space to write this entire book. It really, really helped to #GetShitDone.

References

CHAPTER 1

The World's Women 2015: Trends and Statistics. United Nations Statistics Division, Department of Economic and Social Affairs.

Heilman, Madeline E., and Julie J. Chen. "Same Behavior, Different Consequences: Reactions to Men's and Women's Altruistic Citizenship Behavior." *Journal of Applied Psychology* 90, no. 3 (2005): 431–41.

19th Amendment to the U.S. Constitution, Library of Congress. https://www.loc.gov/rr/program/bib/ourdocs/Images/41stat362.pdf.

Hegewisch, Ariane, M. Phil, and Emma Williams-Baron. "The Gender Wage Gap by Occupation 2016; and by Race and Ethnicity." Institute for Women's Policy Research. April 4, 2017.

Planned Parenthood. "The Birth Control Pill: A History." Last updated June 2015. https://www.plannedparenthood.org/files/1514/3518/7100/Pill_History_FactSheet.pdf.

Jabr, Ferris. "Why Your Brain Needs More Downtime." *Scientific American*. October 15, 2013. https://www.scientificamerican.com/article/mental-downtime.

Ericcson, Anders K. "The Influence of Experience and Deliberate Practice of the Development of Superior Expert Performance" in *The Cambridge Handbook of Expertise and Expert Performance*. Cambridge: Cambridge University Press, 2006.

CHAPTER 2

Mulvey, Laura. "Visual Pleasure and Narrative Cinema." *Screen* 16, no. 3 (October 1975): 6–18.

Grippo, Karen P., and Melanie S. Hill. "Self-objectification, habitual body monitoring and body dissatisfaction in older European American women: Exploring age and feminism as moderators." *Body Image* 5, no. 2 (June 2008): 173–82. doi:10.1016/j.bodyim.2007.11.003.

Mintz, Laurie. "Stop Spectatoring: Mindfulness to Enhance Sexual Pleasure." *Psychology Today*. Posted March 29, 2013. https://www.psychologytoday.com/blog/stress-and -sex/201303/stop-spectatoring-mindfulness-enhance-sexual-pleasure.

Ainley, Vivien. "Body Conscious? Interoceptive Awareness, Measured by Heartbeat Perception, Is Negatively Correlated with Self-Objectification." *PLOS ONE*. February 6, 2013.

McGilchrist, Iain. *The Master and His Emissary: The Divided Brain and the Making of the Western World*. New Haven, CT: Yale University Press, 2012.

Hanh, Thich Nhat. "Five Steps to Mindfulness." Mindful.org. August 23, 2010. https:// www.mindful.org/five-steps-to-mindfulness.

CHAPTER 3

Kanter, Rosabeth Moss. *Men and Women of the Corporation*. New York: Basic Books, 1993.

Heilman, Madeline E., and Julie Chen. "Same Behavior, Different Consequences: Reactions to Men's and Women's Altruistic Citizenship Behavior." *Journal of Applied Psychology* 90, no. 3 (2005): 431–41.

Hochschild, Arlie Russell. *The Managed Heart: Commercialization of Human Feeling*. Berkeley and Los Angeles, CA: University of California Press, 2012.

Schumann, Katrina, and Michael Ross. "Why Women Apologize More Than Men: Gender Differences in Thresholds for Perceiving Offensive Behavior." *Sage Journals* 21, no. 11 (September 2010): 1649–55.

Tannen, Deborah. *Talking from 9 to 5: Women and Men at Work*. New York: William Morrow, 2013.

Bennett, Jessica. "I'm Sorry, But Women Really Need to Stop Apologizing." *Time*. June 18, 2014. http://time.com/2895799/im-sorry-pantene-shinestrong.

Friedman, Ann. "Can We Just, Like, Get Over the Way Women Talk?" *The Cut*. July 9, 2015. https://www.thecut.com/2015/07/can-we-just-like-get-over-the-way-women -talk.html.

CHAPTER 4

Status of Women in the States. Institute for Women's Policy Research. https://statusof womendata.org/explore-the-data.

Rosin, Hanna. *The End of Men: And the Rise of Women*. New York: Riverhead Books, 2012.

———. "New Data on the Rise of Women." TED Talk, 2010. https://www.youtube .com/watch?v=7ZymFMmpOa0.

Dreyer, Kate. "Women Spend More Time Social Networking Than Men Worldwide." *comScore*. December 22, 2011. https://www.comscore.com/Insights/Data-Mine /Women-Spend-More-Time-Social-Networking-than-Men-Worldwide.

Collins, Rebecca L. "For Better or Worse: The Impact of Upward Social Comparison on Self-Evaluations." *Psychological Bulletin* 119 (January 1996): 51–69.

Morris, David Z. "New French Law Bars Work Email After Hours." *Fortune*. January 1, 2017. http://fortune.com/2017/01/01/french-right-to-disconnect-law.

Hwong, Connie. "Chart of the Week: How Do We Spend Our Time Online?" *Verto Analytics*. November 24, 2016. http://www.vertoanalytics.com/chart-of-the-week -how-do-we-spend-our-time-online.

Huang, Chiungjung. "Internet Use and Psychological Well-Being: A Meta-Analysis." *Cyberpsychology, Behavior, and Social Networking* 13, no. 3 (June 2010): 241–49.

Denti, Leif, et al. "Sweden's Largest Facebook Study." University of Gothenburg, Gothenburg Research Institute, 2012.

Primack, Brian A., et al. "Use of Multiple Social Media Platforms and Symptoms of Depression and Anxiety: A Nationally Representative Study Among U.S. Young Adults." *Computers in Human Behavior* 69 (April 2017): 1–9.

Pénard, Thierry, Nicolas Poussing, and Raphael Suire. "Does the Internet Make People Happier?" *Journal of Socio-Economics* 46 (2013): 105–16.

CHAPTER 5

Macnamara, Brooke N., David Z. Hambrick, and Frederick L. Oswald. "Deliberate Practice and Performance in Music, Games, Sports, Education, and Professions." *Psychological Science* 25, no. 8 (2014): 1608–18.

Hofmann, Wilhelm, et al. "Yes, But Are They Happy? Effects of Trait Self-Control on Affective Well-Being and Life Satisfaction." *Journal of Personality* 82, no. 4 (2014): 265–77. doi:10.1111/jopy.12050.

CHAPTER 6

Vanderkam, Laura. "The Busy Person's Lies." *New York Times*. May 13, 2016.

CHAPTER 7

Vanderkam, Laura. *What the Most Successful People Do Before Breakfast: A Short Guide to Making Over Your Mornings—and Life*. New York: Portfolio, 2012.

Ackerman, Jennifer. *Sex Sleep Eat Drink Dream: A Day in the Life of Your Body*. New York: Mariner Books, 2008.

Oswald, Andrew, J., Eugenio Proto, and Daniel Sgroi. "Happiness and Productivity." IZA Discussion Paper no. 4645 (December 2009).

Barker, Eric. "Here's the Schedule Very Successful People Follow Every Day." *The Week*. July 23, 2014. http://theweek.com/articles/445444/heres-schedule-successful-people-follow-every-day.

Medina, John. *Brain Rules: 12 Principles for Surviving and Thriving at Work, Home, and School*. Seattle, WA: Pear Press, 2008.

Perry, Christopher G. R., et al. "High-Intensity Aerobic Interval Training Increases Fat and Carbohydrate Metabolic Capacities in Human Skeletal Muscle." *Applied Physiology, Nutrition, and Metabolism* 33, no. 6 (2008): 1112–23.

Cirillo, Francesco. *The Pomodoro Technique: The Acclaimed Time-Management System That Has Transformed How We Work*. New York: Crown Business, 2013.

Gifford, Julia. "The Rule of 52 and 17; It's Random, But It Ups Your Productivity." *The Muse*. https://www.themuse.com/advice/the-rule-of-52-and-17-its-random-but-it-ups-your-productivity.

Lang, Susan S. "When Workers Heed Computer's Reminder to Take a Break, Their Productivity Jumps, Cornell Study Finds." *Cornell Chronicle*. September 24, 1999. http://news.cornell.edu/stories/1999/09/onscreen-break-reminder-boosts-productivity.

Hillman, Charles H., et al. "The Effect of Acute Treadmill Walking on Cognitive Control and Academic Achievement in Preadolescent Children." *Neuroscience*. February 3, 2009. doi:10.1016/j.neuroscience.2009.01.057.

CHAPTER 8

Oswald, Andrew J., Eugenio Proto, and Daniel Sgroi. "Happiness and Productivity." *Journal of Labor Economics* 33, no. 4 (October 2015).

Fowler, James H., and Nicholas A. Christakis. "Dynamic Spread of Happiness in a Large Social Network: Longitudinal Analysis Over 20 Years in the Framingham Heart Study." *BMJ*. December 5, 2008.

Hatfield, Elaine, John T. Cacioppo, and Richard L. Rapson. *Emotional Contagion.* Cambridge: Cambridge University Press, 1994.

TalentSmart. "About Emotional Intelligence." http://www.talentsmart.com/about/emotional-intelligence.php.

Baxter, Judith. "Survival or Success? A Critical Exploration of the Use of 'Double-Voiced Discourse' by Women Business Leaders in the UK." *Discourse & Communications* 5, no. 3 (2011): 231–45.

CHAPTER 9

Zeigarnik, Bluma. "On Finished and Unfinished Tasks." *Psychologische Forschung*, 1927.

CHAPTER 10

Onyemaechi, Chinenye. "Recognizing Burnout in Women as We Continue to 'Lean In.'" Psychiatry.org. March 8, 2016. https://www.psychiatry.org/news-room/apa-blogs /apa-blog/2016/03/recognizing-burnout-in-women-as-we-continue-to-lean-in.

Weil, Andrew. "Video: Breathing Exercises: 4-7-8 Breath." https://www.drweil.com/videos -features/videos/breathing-exercises-4-7-8-breath.

National Sleep Foundation. "Lack of Sleep Is Affecting Americans, Finds the National Sleep Foundation." December 2014. https://sleepfoundation.org/media-center/press -release/lack-sleep-affecting-americans-finds-the-national-sleep-foundation.